POWER OF
ICU

The End of Student Apathy...
Reviving Engagement &Responsibility

Danny Hill
Dr. Jayson Nave

Text Copyright © *2009*
Danny Hill
Jayson Nave

Cover Artwork Copyright © *2009*
Dennis Auth
www.DennisAuth.com

Cover Design by
Creative Light
www.CreativeLightAgency.com

Cover Art Director
Jose Barcita
www.barcita.com

Book Design and Editing by
Wesley A. Lombardo

Published by
NTLB Publishing
the Educational Imprint of
Southland Books

Thank you to
David Rankin & Maggie Duncan
at Back Home Printing

ISBN
978-0-9823984-3-2

Learn more online at
PowerOfICU.com

MANUFACTURED IN THE UNITED STATES OF AMERICA

PLEASE KNOW
It's not about you:
It's about children learning.

It has never been about you,
and it never will be about you!

Remember why you began
a career in education:
Your love for children and learning

If you believe it, you can do it—
You CAN have EVERY student
turn in EVERY assignment

Danny Hill
Dr. Jayson Nave

WE HAD THE SAME PROBLEM

Encouragement, rewards, punishment, and motivational speeches: nothing worked. It seemed that not doing an assignment was the "in" thing to do. Students' flippant attitude when announcing "I didn't do my homework" would make teachers' blood boil. As the principal, I would be called in out of frustration to deliver an ultimatum: "If you don't do your work, then..." I would fill in the blank with whatever sounded good that day. Things like "you'll never get a job" or maybe "you'll end up failing" would roll off my tongue year after year, and still they never flinched. "We care more about you passing than you do" was another great line, but their eyes and sometimes their mouths simply agreed. The term "Student Apathy" seemed too simple compared to the enormous real-life frustration we felt every single day of the school year. If this were a physical tumor, instead of our medicine reducing the tumor, it seemed to grow larger and more dangerous each year. After 25 years in education, I had resigned myself to the accepted paradigm that we just cannot reach all of them.

Then we changed. All of our students now do every assignment, they never argue with us, they turn in most of their work on time, and they know they will have to redo sloppy work, so they rarely turn in garbage anymore. I NEVER give the old speeches. I NEVER beg. I NEVER threaten. I NEVER argue with parents. We NEVER dreamed things could be this easy! Five years ago, we finally acknowledged that the apathetic students were in control. We realized we had nothing to lose. Our successful students would function successfully under any system. Why not take drastic steps? Toni Eubanks from the Southern Regional Education Board (SREB) visited our county in 2004 and made one simple statement that sent us in the right direction: "When you give students a zero or accept low quality work, you are letting them OFF THE HOOK!"

Yes, the foundation piece for our new system is the No Zero policy, and this book is a "HOW TO" book that will help get you started with a No Zero program that will really work. The purpose of this book is to give you a general pattern to follow in making the transition from the old zero-based grading system to the new No Zero system. Many schools leave conferences excited about changing their grading system, but they fail because they underestimate the difficulty involved. Being convinced by research is just the beginning—this book should be able to lead you the rest of the way.

Teachers have been
left alone
to fight the problem of *apathy*
for *too long.*

What Does ICU Stand For?

ICU stands for Intensive Care Unit, just like in the hospital. ICU is a communication tool, a shared, school-wide document that tracks missing student assignments. The document helps teachers and administrators communicate with each other as well as with the students and their parents. Students learn quickly that if they have one missing assignment, their grade is sick and needs attention. Refusing to give zeroes is the foundation of this process, and the ICU list is the first layer of block in building a completely new system.

Why does it work?

Although teachers are the ones in charge of grading, apathetic students often feel powerful and in control. When they seem cocky in announcing, "I don't have my work" it is because they have recruited a small army of support behind them. They have secretly convinced their mom or dad, grandma or grandpa—maybe even all of them—that their teacher is the problem. After recruiting and winning over their guardian, they gather a few friends and their parents, repeating the theme "It's the teacher's fault!" The teacher versus the student actually turns into the teacher versus the student and the student's small army of support. The ICU helps reverse this. Our system quickly builds an army of support behind the teachers, instead of the students, and eventually even the student switches sides.

Why do so many schools fail miserably in trying to shift to the "No Zero" system and end up right back where they started?

Many schools give up because the shift is not just about a change in policy like no longer giving zeroes. Administrators frequently dump this policy on teachers and underestimate the need to build an entirely new system. The new system is about creating tools and opportunities for teachers and students that guide everyone toward learning. The magic bullet in our ICU system is that it disarms the student's small army, in effect leaving them so alone that eventually the student decides to become engaged in the learning process.

The "Build Up" section of this book will show you how to build a small army of support behind the teacher. Teachers have been left alone to fight the problem of apathy for too long. It is impossible for teachers to shift to the No Zero system by themselves. The army of support refers to teachers, parents, coaches, administrators, counselors, band directors, choir directors, and other adults joining forces. It also refers to specific interventions of "extra time" and "extra help." If student apathy is our biggest problem, why do we treat it with a band aid? Our philosophy is to blow it up and drive it out of our schools, never allowing it to return.

What about the "Tear Down" section of this book? Why not just dive right in with the exciting part of building up? The main barrier to building the new system is Teacher Paradigm, the idea of how things have always been done. Before real change can take place, old ideas of how education works have to be torn down and dismantled. Educators are very stubborn and have grown tired of all the "new stuff" and quick-fix solutions that comes from all sides. The director of schools and the principal can say they will no longer give zeroes, but if the teachers don't buy into it, nothing will change. Tearing down allows principals and teachers to take a good look at the traditional zero-based grading system and all of its flaws. Educators are smart, will listen, and will change if they are allowed enough time and given the proper information to see errors in their paradigm. The transition will end in disaster if you assume the "Tear Down" section is unnecessary.

We Do Not Accept Cash

"We do not accept cash, sir," the college-aged man taking my sandwich order at a local restaurant told me as I gave him a $20 bill.

"This is madness! I pay for everything with cash. Don't you want my business? There are plenty of other restaurants..."

Ryan, my twenty one year old nephew stopped me by placing his hand on my shoulder and whispering in my ear, "Let go Uncle Danny, I'll explain later." Still mad as fire, I pulled out my debit card, paid, and took a seat with my son and nephew to wait for the sandwiches. Looking for an explanation, my nephew spoke with a reverence as he explained, "Remember several months ago, when two people were shot and killed while being robbed at a restaurant? After losing two employees over money, the owner decided he would never accept or keep any cash in his restaurant again."

Changing an established paradigm creates anger, emotion, and resistance. In the situation mentioned above, I was ready to walk out and take my business elsewhere, because not taking cash is just "un-American"! What would Dave Ramsey say? My mind kicked into neutral as I tried to decide if I should stay mad or allow the explanation to be enough to cool my attitude. For the rest of the afternoon, my thoughts were spinning, and by the end of the day I was totally convinced that we should all stop carrying cash because it was no longer needed. This is a simple example of a paradigm shift.

The No Zero movement in schools across the country is being met with a few success stories, but mostly anger and failure. CNN recently reported the uproar created in Dallas, Texas, when the administration told schools they could no longer give zeroes as the baseline for most grading habits. Teachers and parents called it "dumbing down" the district while pushing students through the system who haven't earned their way. Teachers' union officials were disgusted and angry because, as stated by Dale Keiszer, President of the National Education Association, "Instead of setting high expectations and high standards and holding to that, we seem to want to lower the bar and give them an excuse not to succeed."

Conferences are popping up all across America showing research findings in favor of No Zero grading policies. Principals are invited frequently to "Failure is Not an Option" workshops, teaching the "Power of the Incomplete" and the "Glasser Quality Schools"approach, which teaches the "not yet" principle. If research shows this is better for our children, why the anger and resistance? If research shows the zero is unfair to students, kills student motivation, and contributes to the high drop out rate, what is the problem? We believe the problem is the small but difficult bridge of how to implement the proper changes. We have "How To" books on topics ranging from losing weight to becoming a millionaire, but nothing on how to move from our present grading system based on giving zero's and averaging grades to the research based "No Zero/Incomplete." This book is written by principals to fellow educators. We believe in educators. We believe educators want to do what is best for all students, but this new paradigm throws a sweeping curve ball at the educational process. Teachers and principals are being told to drop the zero without being given support systems for the new grading philosophy. The assumption by the so-called leaders of education is that the No Zero philosophy is an easy transition. Nothing could be further from the truth. Taking away the zero based grading system is like throwing a bomb into schools. Asking teachers and administrators to throw out the zero and give incompletes instead is like asking them to speak fluent German without enough time or training. What you are about to read is a very practical letter written to you with many down to earth ideas and practical applications to support you and your school. The plan we layout can be followed specifically or very loosely, depending on your schools needs. One of the strongest parts of this plan is its ability to adapt to any school setting. This book is guaranteed to help in transitioning and creating success in developing a culture of learning in which zeroes will become fading memory.

As principals, we are both eyewitnesses to drastic improvements in student attitudes, behavior, and success due to the paradigm shift in grading policies. We are so excited by what we've seen that neither of us can shut up about it. We have been increasingly called upon to speak to schools and school systems sharing this information. The success reported from these schools has been the main encouragement for writing this book. Can you remember how you felt after watching a truly inspirational movie like *Remember the Titans* or *Rudy*? You couldn't wait to tell everybody—"It was great, you have to see it!" Well, that is how we feel, but our feelings go much deeper than just relaying information about a movie. Real lives, real success, restored hope, and improved learning is much better than any book or movie. What we experience each day is awesome, unbelievable, and amazing. As you read this, be aware of your core beliefs, because if you do not want to challenge what you know about how things have always been done, then put this book down immediately. If, however, you know there has to be a better way to reach more students, to truly help students learn and achieve success, then read on.

By the way, how long before everyone stops taking cash?

"I Wanted to Influence Lives"

Why did you go into education? You along with many others would say "I wanted to influence young lives." You wanted to mold and shape lives in hopes that you could give back maybe something you had or did not receive. You wanted to bring light to a sometimes dark world or enhance great talents in hopes of seeing great achievement.

Teaching is a calling, and most of us begin our careers full of enthusiasm and hope. Along the path of education your hopes, dreams, and visions of grandeur were zapped by administrative paperwork, the battle with student's apathetic ways, and the battle with parents. No longer does this have to happen, because this paradigm shift will break the chains that bind you. You will be released to help students in ways that really matter. You will receive the power you have been looking for without the distractions. This can work in your classroom, in your school, and for a school system. Along this path you will encounter many questions, for this is indeed a drastic paradigm shift. You will look at education in a totally different way. You will remove the knife that has been stabbing your students and your parents for years and they will love you for it. You will have questions about enabling students. You will have questions about how much help is too much help. You will have questions about your own endurance and desire to help students. You will face stumbling blocks, but the process is a great part of the cure. You will grow into an instructional leader who is able to help, instruct, communicate, and solve issues. You will grow into more of a teacher than you ever thought you could be, due to the fact that now everything you do is built on the premise of being a servant-hearted and servant-minded teacher.

The "Power of the ICU" will help you form an army of teacher and student support, filled with administrators, teachers, lifeguards, guidance counselors, and parents all focused on helping individual students learn. The adversarial path of education is gone, due to the fact that you will base everything on service and help. Think of the joy you will feel when you are able to focus on instruction and helping students learn, rather than the stress related to student apathy. You will be free to do what you entered education for—to help, guide, instruct, and give hope to so many young prospective adults.

Enjoy the journey—this one is priceless!

TABLE OF CONTENTS

Section I: Tear Down

Section II: Build Up!

Section III: Real Stories

Section IV: What's Next?

Appendix

POWER OF
ICU

TEAR

DOWN!

1

It's Not About You

What's Your Focus in the Classroom?

The young art museum guide's job was to lead people to the paintings, answer their questions, and step out of the way. Initially, he succeeded. He walked the clients to the framed treasures, identified the artists, and stepped out of view. "This is Monet," he would say and move back as people oohed and aahed and asked a question or two. When they were ready, he would lead them to the next masterpiece and repeat the sequence. "This is the work of Rembrandt." He stepped back; they leaned in. He stood; they stared. Simple job. Delightful job. He took great pride in his work.

Too much pride, one might say, for in a short time he forgot his role. He began thinking the people had come to see *him*. Rather than step away from the work of art, he lingered near it. As they oohed and aahed, he smiled. "Glad you like it," he replied, chest lifting, face blushing. He even responded with an occasional "thank you," taking credit for work he didn't do. Visitors disregarded his comments, but they couldn't dismiss his movements. Lingering near a painting was no longer sufficient for the guide. Little by little he inched toward it, initially extending his arm over the frame, then his torso over part of the canvas. Finally, his body blocked the entire piece. People could see him but not the art. He began to conceal the very work he was sent to reveal.

That's when his superior intervened. "This job isn't about you, don't obscure my masterpieces."

—from "It's Not About You!" by Max Lucado, reprinted by permission

In education, the masterpiece is our students, more specifically student learning. Before I speak at schools, I always ask the principal to send me quotes from the teachers I will be addressing. These quotes give excellent insight into the pattern of thinking, the paradigm, among many teachers. Let's look at a few of them to see if some teachers are standing in front of the masterpiece:

"Why should I have to grade the assignment again after I have already graded it once?"

Notice the emphasis on "grade" and "I" with no mention of one of the most important words in education: Learn.

This next statement is kind of harsh, so brace yourself. ***It's not about you!*** What is education about? Is teaching and learning about the students or is it about the teacher? This is a fundamental question every educator will be forced to answer when a school tries to make the transition from a traditional grading scale to a No Zero policy.

An educator's paradigm is wrong if it emphasizes anything besides student learning. Teachers need to be reminded that it's never been about you—and it is never going to be about you—at your school.

"When you don't strictly enforce due dates, students start to feel it really doesn't matter if they do the work or not. The feeling is they can just turn it in later."

In reality this is toxic thinking, especially for young teachers who get little if any information on grading practices while in college. After entering the profession, new teachers often rely on their buddy teacher or whoever was assigned to show them how to set up their grade book. Toni Eubanks, Regional Director of the Southern Regional Education Board (SREB), says "Schools must begin to have conversations with their staffs about the effects of grading practices on students' grades and GPAs. Students with the exact same grades on the exact same assignments might receive a final grade two or even three letter grades different, based on different teachers' grading practices or assignment weighting. These differences usually place unfair emphasis on due dates. Little, if any, direction is provided to teachers in this area. Districts must begin providing teachers with specific training on grading practices, particularly standards-based grading, formative and summative grading differences, and the effects of zeroes on grade averages and GPAs."

"Why should we let kids have more time?"

Teachers who have put forth the effort to change to the ICU system think these comments are hilarious. When a teacher is able to let go of traditional thinking and totally focus on student learning, it is like a veil is being lifted from their eyes. "I have seen a student with the worst home life and no support at all learn to manage all of his assignments on time and all by himself," writes Audrey, a 7th grade math teacher, after three years on the ICU system. "At our school, he [referring to a high-maintenance student] has learned responsibility and will head to high school with a great foundation."

Dr. Gene Bottoms, Executive Vice President for SREB, says "All students will do all assignments if given one thing—enough time."[3] Why are teachers so set on deadlines? Is it because they need to get that grade in that little box in their grade book? Is that the driving force? Teachers need to be able to live under the same restrictions and policies they place on their students. Therefore, following this pat-

Maybe teachers should *forfeit 10% of their pay* for every day something is turned in late or inaccurate to the office.

tern of thinking, teachers should never be given more time to turn in grade reports and other paperwork to their principals. At your school, how many teachers would have lost their jobs if they had to meet every deadline or get the ax? For that matter, would you still be principal at your school if everything had to be turned in on time to the district office?

"We need a deadline for assignments and everybody needs to stick to them!"
Can you hear the pattern of thinking that has been passed down over the years? Let's play with this "the Deadline is the main thing" argument for a moment. In one situation, I sent out an email requesting that teachers be more accurate and timely in turning in their attendance each morning, including a few examples to help clarify the problem. A week later, I sent out another reminder email. It was frustrating, then, later in the week when we called a parent one morning to check on why her son, Nathaniel, was home. Was he sick? Laying out? After several minutes of panic on mom's part, we double checked and Nathaniel was at school and he had even arrived on time. Where was the problem in the system? The problem was that the teacher turned in his attendance report late to the office, creating unnecessary confusion, anxiety, and anger.

Teachers regularly place incredible emphasis on deadlines, especially in high school. Principals will tell you that the teachers who eagerly slap zeroes on their students for not meeting a deadline are frequently the same ones who consistently are late and irresponsible employees. But, of course, all of us are products of the zero-based grading system that has failed for years to "Teach Responsibility."

Deadlines, responsibility, and teacher comfort ("gotta get a grade in that little box") take precedent over students and learning.

Toni Eubanks has worked with states, districts, and schools across the country to help them implement a grading system where failure is not an option. In her workshops, she points out that "a grading system that gives students the 'choice' to not attempt or complete assignments, the 'choice' to not study, fail tests, and just go on, or the 'choice' to turn in work that does not meet grade-level standards, then we are actually teaching students that they will have these choices as an adult." She goes on to say that "In order to get our youth, our future, ready to be successful, hard-working adults, one of the most important skills we must give them is a strong work ethic. A work ethic includes the tenacity to finish a job and do it well. Our current grading system tells many, many students over and over again that they are failures, zeroes, but it does nothing to teach them that failure is not one of their options. We have to teach them that their failure is short-term and then give them opportunities to re-do their efforts and work harder to make it better." She tells participants in her workshop that "when we simply give a grade to their current level of effort instead of requiring them to work harder, study more, and re-do their initial work and re-take tests until they can at least pass, then we are 'letting them off the hook' for learning and setting them up for failure in life."

"This new stuff [the No Zero approach] doesn't work. This too will go away in a few years"

Remember, these real life comments were all collected from teachers who supposedly tried this "new stuff" for less than a year. Have educators been bombarded with so many crazy new ideas that it is difficult to recognize something truly effective when it comes along?

Do secondary teachers know they have some serious problems? How many articles from business magazines and upper-education professors complain the students coming out of high school are not prepared? Politicians complain constantly that spending extra money on education never brings about true reform. We try to fix our dropout numbers with GED, adult high school, and creative record keeping. My wife, Deb, is a high school guidance counselor and has been taught the best way to steer the dropouts to make the numbers look better. Steering a dropout into the adult high school instead of the GED program, for example, doesn't affect numbers as much. While all of these solutions make the problem seem smaller on paper, we still are not addressing our core problem: student apathy. This "new stuff" doesn't cost anything, drastically helps students, and it is here to stay.

"If you get your payment to the water company late, your water is turned off. If you are late on the electric bill, you get disconnected. When students are late on homework and keep getting chances without zeroes, you are teaching them a lie about real life."

Aren't these comments a hoot? Teachers try to use this one all the time—an analogy to real life. This has been covered already, but it is really fun to revisit this because it has absolutely no merit. First of all, the smell of "It's about me" lingers once again. Secondly, "I've got to get that grade in the little box" is nearby. However, just to have a little fun, let's go with it for a minute to check for truth or lies. The water company and the electric company gives you 30 to 60 days to get your payment in before they can legally turn you off. They never send you a notice saying "You have waited too long to pay your bill, therefore you are off the hook and no longer responsible for the payment." In fact, they do exactly what the ICU system does: they send constant reminders. Finding any correlation between our present zero-based grading system and the real world is very difficult. The ICU System teaches responsibility, the students do their work, and we watch them growing into the type of adults who will pay their water bills on time. So, in reality, teachers really are able to get a GRADE into the little box, not just a zero.

One accepted consequence among teachers who deeply believe "everybody needs to stick to these deadlines" is to take off ten points per day for each day the assignment is late. Maybe teachers should forfeit 10% of their pay for every day something is turned in late or inaccurate to the office. Under the present zero system, we are teaching students how to fail by emphasizing deadlines over learning. Dropout rates are horrendous. By letting students off the hook, we have sent the message for many years that you can do nothing and still be taken care of. Isn't that called Enabling?

ICU Notes

2

WHO CREATED THIS GRADING SCALE, ANYWAY?

Shouldn't we know more about the origins of one of the cornerstones of modern education?

Who created the zero-based grading scale? Does anyone really know? Why was it created? Does it help promote learning? In traveling all over and speaking to thousands of teachers, no one yet has known the answers to these questions. So I ask you: Why are so many educators sold out to a system we may have inherited from the three stooges?

Are you prepared to defend a system that nationally allows about a third of the students who enter kindergarten to drop out before graduating from high school? You owe it to yourself, your students, and your parents to take a closer look.

Before the compulsory attendance laws were passed in the late nineteenth and early twentieth centuries, grading and reporting was very informal. The teacher reported students' learning progress orally to parents, usually during home visits. The bottom line is our present grading system was born out of necessity due to the drastic increase in student enrollment and the resulting enormous increase in teacher workloads. It was not added because it was found to enhance learning. In reality, grading and reporting are not essential to the instruction and assessment process.

Teacher Talk

"I remember before we switched to the ICU system, several times throughout the year, going to my board and showing my classes how devastating just one zero was to their grade. I would practically beg them to do their work. I never even considered using a different pattern for grading. Now I am more confident my student grades are a much better reflection of their learning. We will never go back to that other system of giving zeroes."

—Leslie, middle school social studies teacher with twelve years in the classroom

> If the only tool we have is a
>
> # *hammer*
>
> then we tend to see every problem as a
>
> # *nail.*
>
> —Abraham Maslow

Dr. Robert Canady, Professor at the University of Virginia, states "The threat of a low grade is more likely to motivate high-achieving students than low-achieving students." So why do we use the devastating zero to threaten the struggling learner when the only students the zero affect are the top students. The top student does not really need you, and if you don't believe this ask some of the students who are taking online classes from home.

Dr. Canady also states "There is little or no evidence that repeated failure makes people more responsible." Stop grading responsibility and behavior; it does not coexist with learning. Allowing the zero as an option for student grades, or even allowing extremely low grades, is in direct contrast to teaching, learning, and a standards-based curriculum. So why are you running a school with grading and curriculum processes that contradict each other?

ICU Notes

THE LONE ZERO

The impact of a single grade

Many teachers use the zero as a weapon of last resort. Think about the common language associated with our zero-based grading system. Think of all the times you've said "I'm just going to have to give you a zero," or if you're really nice "Sorry, but I'm just going to have to give you a zero." This negative motivator is truly a dead end for the teacher, the student, the parent, and the school. The action of allowing a zero is like massaging a dead body: teachers are putting out all of the effort, but the system has already killed the body. It is like a dead end road, and you might as well change direction.

The negative effect of assigning zeros is greatly magnified if combined with the common practice of averaging scores to attain students' overall course grade. A single zero leaves students little chance for success because it drastically skews the average. For instance, imagine a student earned the grades listed below:

85—88—92—83—97—84—88—96—99—93

Without adding them up, just estimate: Is this an A, B, C, D, or F student?

Teacher Talk

"We can remember when we had a group of boys years ago who decided to just shut down on us. We chewed and threatened them the entire second semester. Although we tried to sound like we were in control, in reality we were helpless. We ended up moving them on, knowing they did not earn it."

—*Marilyn and Mike have seen it all in their combined sixty five years teaching, and they are both excited about our new culture.*

> **"A zero is seldom an accurate reflection of what a student has learned. If a grade is to represent how well students have learned or mastered a standard, then the practice of assigning zeroes clearly misses the mark."**
>
> **—Barry Raebeck**

You would probably say this student is a B student or maybe a low A student. The student has a 90.5 average. Now, pretend the student missed a deadline and take out the 84 and replace it with a 0.

85—88—92—83—97—0—88—96—99—93

You would probably still believe that this is an A or B student, or at least agree that the student should receive an A or B based on the impression you get from looking at the grades. One zero, however, dropped this solid B student eight points to a C. There are two problems with the traditional paradigm. One, the student is not held accountable for learning the material, and secondly, it is mathematically impossible for the student to earn what is truly a reflection of their learning. Forgiving teachers realize that everyone misses something sometimes and will solve the problem of the one low score by dropping the lowest grade. Under the ICU system we do not drop the lowest grade because that is not what would happen in real life and it wouldn't teach responsibility. Instead, the ICU gives extra time, support, and reminders to get the assignment in, not just to put a number in a box, but to ASSESS what has been LEARNED.

Are you still ready to defend a system that grades responsibility, deadlines, and behavior? Please think about what you are doing. Are you willing to look at a different method that is proving to teach responsibility by never letting a student off the hook?

ICU Notes

QUIT FOOLING YOURSELF

A passing grade alone does not indicate success or failure

"We are lowering our grading standard when we take away the zeroes" is one of the war cries being repeated by people in opposition to the No Zero grading system. Is there really such a high standard with the current grading system, or do teachers consistently massage student grades to cut down on the number of failures? Grade massaging is rampant under the zero-based grading system in a variety of ways.

Grades are Curved. One of the most common massage techniques is to curve grades. This practice has been around for years and it sets a very low standard because the end result is to give students points they didn't earn. If 90 is the highest grade on a test, it becomes the starting point for "curving" the rest of the grades upward. Does this make sense? Giving students points sounds like Enabling!

Drop the lowest grade. Why? How does this prepare students for the real world? It is the most commonly used form of grade massaging and is only accepted by teachers because it has been around for a long time. Under the ICU system, students redo poor quality work and they restudy and retake tests. The new system correlates with "real life," whereas the old system only operates in the vacuum of schools. Dropping the lowest grade sets a very low expectation for the student. Dropping the lowest grade sounds like Enabling!

Don't give less than a 50/60. Many principals and even some school systems tell teachers to not "give" students less than a 50 or 60 on any given assignment or test. Therefore, students doing poor quality work and even the students turning in no work are "given" 50 or 60 points. We should never give students points. Giving students points is ... .Enabling!

"I guess I'll just have to give you a zero." Students who are already apathetic could care less about getting a zero, so we actually sound ridiculous when we say this. Students look at us like, "Okay, so give it to me, but *please* just leave me alone!" We know this for a fact because we heard this all the time when we adopted the ICU at our school. In sticking to the mission that "All students will do every assignment," students will beg you to just leave them alone. Letting students off the hook for an assignment is Enabling!

"You are too old to be here." What do you do with the students who sit around and do nothing all year, but who are too old to keep in a certain grade? We cannot have an 18 year old 8th grader. These students have traditionally been moved on without earning their way. Moving students on without earning their way... isn't that called Enabling?

Once again, we are "giving" students something for doing nothing. DEAD END!

We don't want them back next year. Every time this one is brought up in front of a group of teachers, everyone laughs. It is sort of a best kept secret among educators who have been around a while. For one example of how it works, at a large middle school every year the principal and the teachers gathered to assess failures. The principal would begin with a very firm stance. "Give me the name of

Teacher Talk

"We used to get together at the end of the year and work together as a team to try to find ways to move them on. It was hard to explain this to the new teachers. You can't have an eighteen year old in eighth grade so we didn't see any other option. That never happens anymore with our new system everyone earns their way."

—*Mike, who has been in education for twenty eight years including coaching, high school administration, elementary and middle school administration, and presently eighth grade Algebra and pre-Algebra.*

"We used to send students to the high school whether they were crippled, cross eyed, or crazy! That never happens anymore. They grow responsible, feel good about themselves, and leave here with hope and confidence."

—*Linda, a teacher and counselor for thirty six years.*

any student who made below a 69 and they will be retained." First year teachers were impressed with the high standard of expectation they were hearing. Within minutes, because the number of failures was growing out of control, he would say lets change that, anyone below a 67 will be retained. He would then stop and lower it to 65, then 63, then after two to three hours of this process the baseline finally got to 57 before breaking for lunch. After lunch and discussion with assistant principals, he had settled on this baseline for failures "Give me the names of anyone who did not pass physical education, for they do not deserve to pass."

Are you laughing now? However, everyone agrees some students are moved on to the next grade because they just cannot stomach the thought of having them for another year. *We do not want them back* means *they do not earn their way,* which is Enabling!

Although there are other forms of "grade massaging," if we combine all of the above we have this scenario. Classmates sit in class with these students and hear the teacher fuss and threaten all year. They watch their peers do little or nothing and hear teachers tell them, "You will have to repeat next year if you don't …" Then, when the next school year starts, those same students magically appear sitting next to them in the next grade level. This scenario repeats itself for several years until the middle school dumps them on the high school. Enabling one student by giving them something they did not earn will attract more students each year.

The zero-based grading system is a failure because it gives students points, moves students on without earning their way, and ends quite often with a high dropout rate, but what happens in high school? Teachers offer it up and if the student does not get it, then it is the students fault. High school teachers are the most resistant to change. They believe deeply that students should be old enough, mature enough, responsible enough, and care enough to meet all deadlines. If a student is immature or irresponsible they are given "what they deserve." Many times this leads to dropping out, another DEAD END!

ICU Notes

HIGH SCHOOL CONVERT

A skeptic convinced

In the summer of 2002, I was riding back from Louisville with my assistant principal and another teacher. They were both very excited about a session they had attended at the *High Schools That Work Conference* entitled "The Power of I." According to the presenter, students should never receive zeroes, but should be given an "I" for "Incomplete" until the work is completed. As my traveling companions explained the program to me, I felt very defensive. The word "enabling" kept coming to mind, and I didn't want to be an "enabler." I vividly remembered my college professors who would accept no excuses for late work and wondered how I would have ever gotten my diploma if my high school years had conditioned me to expect unlimited chances. I laid out my arguments: we need to teach the importance of deadlines; we are doing students a disservice by making them believe that they will have unlimited time to complete tasks in college or in their careers. We want students to become responsible adults; by letting them ignore deadlines we are failing to teach responsibility. Some work is time-critical; if we give them unlimited time to complete it, the value of the assignment is diminished or lost if we have moved on to another topic in class. Finally, I stressed the fact that other teachers would never accept an idea like this because the grading of excessive late work would mean so much extra work for them.

By the time we returned to school, the excitement of the summer conference had waned and the idea of the "Power of the I" was never elevated beyond the discussion in the car. Every year we heard variations of this idea at the same summer conference, but every year these concepts were dismissed as too difficult to implement or not right for us. The arguments I had outlined in the car were the same arguments most of the teachers made when discussing the No Zero policy.

The high school soon found itself on the target list for No Child Left Behind due to substandard graduation rates. The school scrambled for a solution, concerned about apathetic students and high dropout percentages. Under pressure to keep our failure rates low, many teachers had to get creative with grades. To lower the number of students who would fail my class because of not completing their homework, I found myself eliminating nightly homework assignments. This re-

I was one of the *most vocal opponents* of the No Zero policy, and I regularly *voiced my concern*

sulted in fewer grades and, consequently, fewer zeroes for me to deal with. Strangely enough, I had identified the correct problem, but I was taking the wrong approach to fix it. I should not have to eliminate the assignment in order to eliminate the zero… I should eliminate the ability of the student to skip the assignment! The solution was right there, but I was too blinded by my "high school thinking" to consider it.

The perception of Southside's "no zeroes" policy was overwhelmingly negative at the high school level. We already had problems with apathetic students; what was going to happen when the Southside students became conditioned to having unlimited opportunities to do their work? This would make our failure rate even worse as we would undoubtedly have to deal with students who had no concept of "deadline" and who expected teachers to spoon-feed them through their high school careers. High school teachers are too busy to spoon-feed. We heard that Southside did not let students fail. To us that meant lower expectations; they must be "giving" grades—how else could you not let students fail? So we believed the quality of students that would be coming out of Southside would get consistently worse as they passed students on who should have been retained. I was one of the most vocal opponents of the No Zero policy, and I regularly voiced my concern that we would be the ones forced to deal with these students who had not earned their eighth grade diplomas and had been conditioned to be irresponsible. I believed we had a tough road ahead to get these students ready for college when they were so far behind to begin with.

In the spring of 2007, I wrote my thesis for my Ed.S. on the way freshman academy structure affects the success of a freshman academy program. I followed the academic progress of students who had been in freshman academy at Wilson Central compared to those who had not. In my research, I looked at the lowest 100 freshmen at Wilson Central over the last five years, and I was surprised to find that only about 5% of those students came from Southside. Contrary to my beliefs about the preparation those students were receiving, Southside was producing our top academic achievers. This discovery contributed to my decision to send my daughter to Southside in the fall of 2007. Over the course of that school year, my work with Wilson Central's advisory committee led me to a closer examination of the No Zero policy at Southside. I became more familiar with the rationale behind it and developed a more thorough understanding of the way the program worked. Although I understood it much better, I was still not in complete agreement. The need to teach responsibility still nagged at me, and that voice in my head still whispered "enabling."

In the summer of 2008, I made a radical decision to leave Wilson Central and teach at Southside so that I could be near my daughter. I understood the implications of this decision: I would have to "walk the walk." I knew I would have to accept late work. I knew I could not give students zeroes if they came in without their homework. I understood that I would be calling parents, listing students on the ICU list, and working with them after hours to help them get what they thought they couldn't get. I was okay with this because I really wanted to work at Southside, but I still worried that I might be contributing to students experiencing high school culture shock and failure at life.

Boy, was I wrong. Within my first few weeks at the school I realized the value of the reteach and retest program. If students didn't understand the material for a test, they are given the opportunity to study harder and try again. How many times had that mantra been beaten into my head as a child: "If at first you don't succeed, try, try again." Why on earth is that idea not taken to heart by educators everywhere? Don't students deserve the opportunity to succeed, even if it takes more than one try? When I realized this, it was a short leap to the No Zero policy. Students should be able to "try, try again" on every assignment, not just tests. I thought about the number of times that I am imperfect and need some extra time to get something done. No one tells me it's "now or never"—instead, I am expected to do it right. The same courtesy should be given to students. I was also amazed at how infrequently I have to give them that courtesy. I believe students have resigned themselves to the fact that they will have to get the work done, so they might as well do it on time. The result is amazing – I am not overwhelmed with late work to grade; in fact, I have less now than I did at the high school. But the best part is that students are learning in spite of themselves! We are not detracting from their sense of responsibility; we are making them more responsible by reinforcing the idea that poor quality work is unacceptable. Knowing this now, I am confident that we are sending students to high school prepared for what they will encounter and well-equipped to excel at high school work. However, I am sad that I was such a vocal opponent of the "Power of the I" when I was at the high school level because it would have helped. I now realize that this program is the best defense against low graduation rates. If we don't allow them to fail, they won't fail. It's that simple. Now when I hear the voice whisper "enabling," I know it really means something entirely different: ***I am enabling these students to succeed!***

—Randi taught high school English for eleven years before moving into the ICU system as a seventh grade Reading teacher.

ICU Notes

CULTURAL INCONSISTENCIES

Are you sending the right message?

Why do students enter kindergarten excited about school and start showing signs of apathy towards their school work around fourth or fifth grade, and why does it increase each year thereafter? This is a difficult progression to see because very few K-12 schools exist. Most teachers in K-8 schools will agree there are significantly more apathetic students in fourth grade than kindergarten and more in eighth grade than in fourth. High schools have a built-in system of weeding out apathetic students. Students don't do their work, don't get the credit, fall behind, and then they drop out. Everyone agrees that dropout rates are too high, but this weak, traditional system continues on. How do excited kindergartners eventually become dropouts? Teachers, especially in secondary schools, claim "We are doing everything we can!" This statement is actually true under the zero-based grading system because the zero is a dead end.

Have you ever noticed the "Cultural Inconsistencies" or inconsistent messages we send our students during their K-12 experience?

"What did you learn today, Amy?" This is a routine question all parents and teachers ask kindergarten students. Around third/fourth grade this emphasis on learning changes and students are helpless. Parents and teachers begin to ask, "What did you make on that test, Amy?" We begin to steer students away from the most important reason they attend school: to learn! For the next nine to ten years, there is a consistent loud voice coming from adults: "What did you MAKE?"

When did grades become more important than learning? When did doing the work and meeting a deadline become more important than learning? This is a huge and very specific shift in emphasis, and teachers *can* and *must* stop it. How does this affect apathy? Research shows that learning is motivational for everyone, while grades alone only motivate our top students. Teachers in the upper grades routinely put grades on assignments and tests and then move on. This is in total contrast to what primary grade teachers do. The assumption of most secondary teachers is that they, the students, should have gotten it. "I covered it, even went over what would be on the test. They just didn't try."

Ask teachers approximately how many grades they have each grading period

Which statement do you most agree with?

My job as a teacher is to be sure my students learn the standards I have been given to teach.

Or

My job as a teacher is to teach the standards and hope they get it.

One of the main jobs of the ICU program is to remind teachers and students that

learning is at the heart of education.

and it is hilarious to hear the wide range. Some teachers claim they have been told in the past they should have at least two solid grades per week. Emphasis on a certain "quantity of grades" has no educational basis and sends an inconsistent message to our students that it's no longer about learning. In trying to have "lots of grades," are teachers attempting to help students pass? Routinely, a large number of grades are averaged and this average then becomes the implied percentage of learning. Are these grades a reflection of learning, doing, or meeting deadlines? The way a teacher looks at grades says a lot about what is truly important to that teacher.

Most kindergarten classes do not give grades, middle school and high school classes generally give lots of grades, and college classes usually give just a couple of grades for the entire course. Should we take the kindergarten emphasis on learning and make it the consistent main emphasis all the way to 12th grade, or do we bring the emphasis on grades, deadlines, and doing your work down to kindergarten? Obviously, if we drag the emphasis on grades and doing your work thinking down we would undoubtedly drag student apathy down with it. How many first graders would shut down and quit trying if we told them "If you can't read by Thanksgiving, then you're lazy! We can't slow down the rest of the class, so we have to move on without you." The ICU model will fix this over time because it leads you back to emphasis on learning, which keeps our message to students clear and consistent.

Kindergarten teachers consistently check for understanding and find ways to be sure all students learn. Students are supposed to learn their ABC's and how to count to 100, for example. Teachers assess where the child is and then provide extra time and extra help to be sure their students learn the standards that they have been given to teach. During the child's upper elementary years, teachers begin to buy into

What is the School Culture?

in Most K-12 Schools

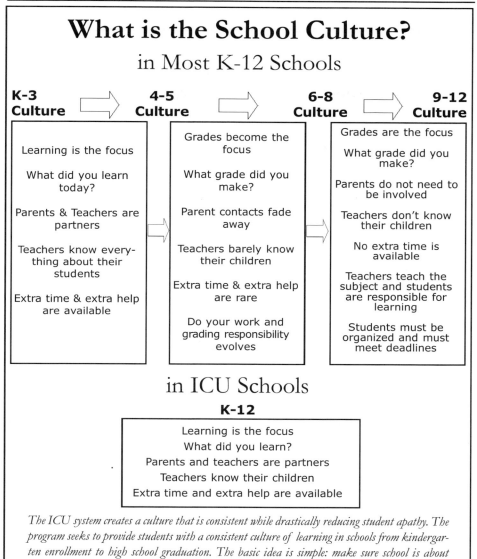

K-3 Culture	4-5 Culture	6-8 Culture	9-12 Culture
Learning is the focus	Grades become the focus		Grades are the focus
What did you learn today?	What grade did you make?		What grade did you make?
Parents & Teachers are partners	Parent contacts fade away		Parents do not need to be involved
Teachers know everything about their students	Teachers barely know their children		Teachers don't know their children
Extra time & extra help are available	Extra time & extra help are rare		No extra time is available
	Do your work and grading responsibility evolves		Teachers teach the subject and students are responsible for learning
			Students must be organized and must meet deadlines

in ICU Schools

K-12

Learning is the focus
What did you learn?
Parents and teachers are partners
Teachers know their children
Extra time and extra help are available

The ICU system creates a culture that is consistent while drastically reducing student apathy. The program seeks to provide students with a consistent culture of learning in schools from kindergarten enrollment to high school graduation. The basic idea is simple: make sure school is about learning from the first day to the last.

the thinking that the child's learning is the child's responsibility. The ICU system provides extra time and extra help, which is the norm in the primary grades. This develops a culture of learning in which teachers take responsibility for student learning and students begin to return to active engagement in school.

When asked for a job description, most lower-grade teachers say, "I teach children," while too many upper-grade teachers say, "I teach math" or "I teach science" or "I teach social studies." This is another significant cultural inconsistency because it represents a very unhealthy paradigm. "I teach math" clearly sends the message that the subject is more important than the child. Teachers come into the profession wanting to help students, but are coerced into believing the subject is more important than the student. This coercion is driven by the strong emphasis on test scores by the state and federal government. The ICU system is student centered, raises expectations, and improves overall achievement. Of course we need math majors to teach secondary math, but this does not excuse shifting the emphasis off of our children. We go into education to help children, and then we get sidetracked by these accepted cultural inconsistencies which fuel student apathy.

Primary teachers believe it is extremely important to include parents in their child's education. Secondary teachers buy into the paradigm that the older the student is, the less they need to develop a relationship with parents. Calling parents is routine to primary teachers, but the idea of calling parents when their child is missing assignments or doing poorly is anything but routine with secondary teachers. The battle cry is either, "I have too many students" or "They are old enough and should be responsible enough." The truth is that most parents care just as much about their high school freshman as they do about their kindergartner. Parents routinely ask their children "How are you doing in school?" or "How are your grades?" Without communication from teachers, it's often too late to make a difference by the time report cards arrive at home. Would you not appreciate a call from your son or daughter's Freshman English teacher saying, "Your son, Zach, did not turn in his paper today; will you be sure he gets it to me tomorrow?" The top secondary teachers already do this with success, but their colleagues would rather see the student fail or drop out than to even give it a try. What if kindergarten teachers took on the paradigm that "It's not my job to call parents. If little Sally is old enough to come to school, then she is old enough to be responsible for her school work"? Once again, if we bring the secondary paradigm down to the primary grades, we will drag student apathy down with it. On the other hand, the ICU system will bring the primary teachers' paradigm upward and student motivation will rise up with it.

In the lower grades, when students are still excited about learning, teachers do not use grades as punishment. Another cultural inconsistency occurs in the upper grades as teachers increasingly grade responsibility and timeliness of assignments turned in. A parent whose child attends school in California recently shared, "My

Teacher Talk

"After 36 years as a professional educator, I am totally convinced that a school's culture determines the degree to which students succeed or fail. Our culture is composed of "solution people" who create a unique learning environment in which teachers teach children, not just subjects or facts."
—Dr. Fred Wheeler, former Georgia State Championship basketball coach who came out of retirement to teach and coach at Southside Middle School

> *One of the easiest ways for human beings to*
> *AVOID the RESPONSIBILITY of FAILURE*
> *is to* **QUIT TRYING!**
>
> —Dr. Robert Canady

child is immature for a 7th grader, but very intelligent. At his school, if he turns in an assignment late, it is an automatic 50 points off of his grade. By the time I learn about the assignment, it is too late." The accepted paradigm among many is the more points you take off per day, the more students will be motivated to turn in assignments on time. Did anybody read the true story of the Japanese elementary child who was struggling to get to school on time? A tardy policy was in place to motivate students to be on time. A gate would close when the bell rang and then students were not allowed in. The rationale behind the plan was that tougher was better. The gate was a huge iron gate and the little girl was so frantic to get in on time that the gate closed on her head and killed her. Was tougher more successful? Does subtracting more points bring positive results? If you take off fifty points, more students will turn their work in on time than only subtracting five? Stop believing in lies. These policies are not built on research, but they are allowed to continue to hurt our students. We owe our students a consistent learning culture from kindergarten through high school.

Giving zeros represents the greatest cultural inconsistency of all. Allowing the students the option of taking a zero or accepting a very low grade is in direct contrast to a standards-based curriculum.. Think about this premise for a minute: Teachers are hired by the Department of Education. The department tells teachers "these are the standards your students must learn." Teachers have assumed for years they have the authority to record "zero learning" for their students. Can a teacher tell a student "You did not meet my deadline, therefore you cannot learn the standard?"

ICU Notes

7

PARADIGM PARALYSIS

If you do things the way you've always done them, you will get the results you've always gotten

How long before everybody stops taking cash? What will thieves steal if there is no longer cash in purses and wallets? If everyone in the family has a personal cell phone, is there a need for landlines? We are already using identification chips to locate lost pets, why not put them in children? Maybe it's already being done! Over ninety years ago, women were jailed for picketing the White House, carrying signs asking for the right to vote. By the end of the night, they were barely alive. Forty prison guards wielding clubs and with their warden's blessing went on a rampage against the 33 women wrongly convicted of 'obstructing sidewalk traffic.' They beat Lucy Burns, chained her hands to the cell bars above her hanging for the night, bleeding and gasping for air. Read about the November 15, 1917 "Night of Terror" and then watch the apathy among women (and men) in the next election. Whenever there is a major shift in our thinking patterns, the change will be met with resistance and anger. The resistance and anger is only multiplied if the shift in thinking is forced on us!

According to John C. Harrison, Program Director of the National Stuttering Project, "a paradigm is a model or a pattern of thinking. It's a shared set of assumptions with how we perceive the world. Paradigms are very helpful because they allow us to develop expectations about what will probably occur based on these assumptions. But when data falls outside our paradigm, we find it hard to see and accept. This is called the Paradigm Effect. And when the paradigm effect is so strong that we are actually prevented from actually seeing what is under our very noses, we are said to be suffering from Paradigm Paralysis." Building the ICU system will take a shift in thinking. There is usually a handful of vocal teachers on every staff who suffer from paradigm paralysis, and they cannot be allowed to destroy the others. Just because they are loud doesn't mean they are right!

Think of challenges to accepted paradigms from the past that created anger, emotion, and resistance but turned out to be the TRUTH. Galileo's assertion that the earth was not the center of the solar system created anger and had him kicked out of the church and imprisoned for speaking the truth. Scientific research clearly shows that smoking causes cancer. Imagine going back in time and telling a group of cowboys that cigarette smoking is harmful to their health—you would be shot! Remember the CNN article previously mentioned concerning the Dallas school system and the anger and the frustration created by the No Zero system which teachers and parents claim is "dumbing down" student expectations. Research clearly states that doing away with the zero-based grading system actually has the opposite effect of raising student expectations. The largest obstacle in changing the culture of your school is making the paradigm shift, because teachers will say, "This is how we have always done it" or "I'm old school." To be truly old school we would need to look at the thinking pattern of teachers in the one room school house. Students remained in a grade level until they learned the material and then advanced to the next grade. If you were twelve years old, but still in the first grade reader, then you stayed in the first grade reader until you mastered it and moved to the second grade reader. The paradigm shift called for in this book is truly a return to the old school thinking pattern where students learn the material and earn their own way to the next level. The ICU system is grounded with research and creates higher expectations and accountability. Are you thinking about this yet? Are you still ready to argue for the zero-based grading system?

ICU Notes

8

THE HOUSE

"It takes a stronger foundation to build a church than an outhouse."

When you begin to implement the ICU program in your school, remember: it depends on a paradigm shift in your thinking. If you continue with the old mindset but just make teachers give 60s or 70s instead of zeroes, it will never work. You have to build a strong foundation from the ground up that is built on the philosophy that learning and not grading is the most important part of a child's education.

As the ICU program in your school begins to transition from Tearing Down to Building Up, the strength of the program's foundation becomes evident. If there's no buy-in from all stakeholders in the school, from teachers and administrators to students and parents, then there will be no real growth or change.

The following two illustrations—The Shack and The Mansion—show two scenarios: the results you get under the traditional, zero-based grading system and the results you can achieve using the ICU system.

The Shack

If you try to simply add on a few components of the ICU program to the same old thinking, you will end up with a paradigm that closely resembles the house below. Would you try to add on to an old, dilapidated shack? Merely adding tools like No Zero grading policies to your existing paradigm has the same effect.

—illustration by Pat Coots' middle school art class

Your Mansion

However, If your administration and staff can commit to the ICU, can commit to student learning, then your house will look like a mansion. It will be a strong structure that can withstand hard times and adapt to changing situations. A program with a strong foundation can constantly adapt and evolve, adding new components as needs arise. Such a mansion has a place for all students.

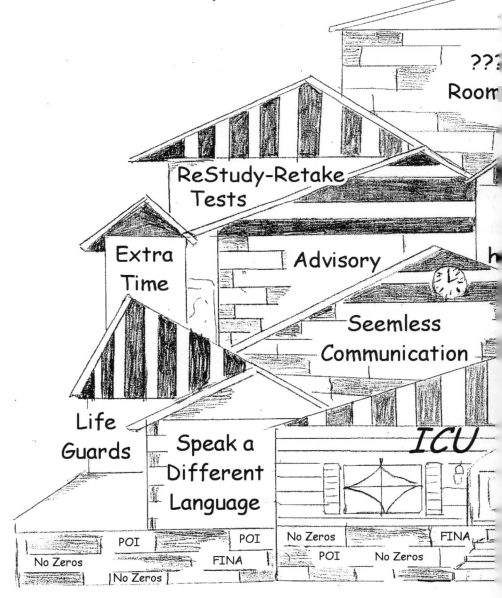

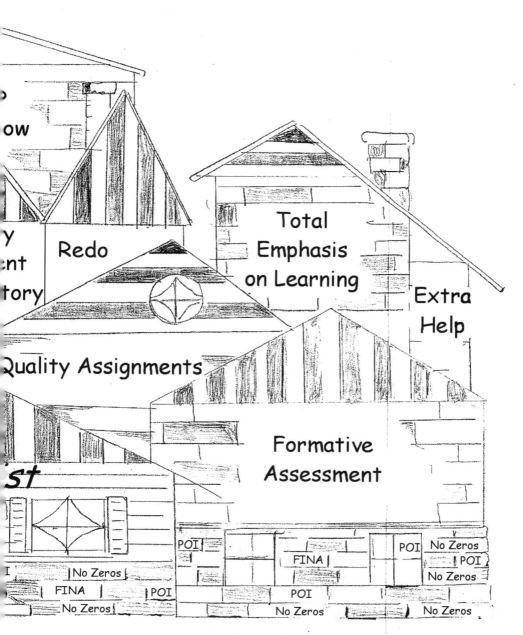

—*illustration by Tyler Sullivan, middle school art student*

POWER OF
ICU

BUILD
UP!

9

WISE LEADERSHIP: TEACH A PARADIGM SHIFT

Success depends on effectively leading teachers to a new philosophy of learning

Be stubborn about pursuing the No Zero system but DO NOT FORCE IT ON YOUR TEACHERS! There is no doubt that the biggest mistake being made in schools and school districts is moving too fast and underestimating the importance of teacher resistance. Nobody likes to have something shoved down their throats without time to think about it. If you drive a very nice Honda but your boss made you switch to a Toyota, it would bring about a reaction just because it is being forced on you. Zig Ziglar says *to react* to something is bad, but *to respond* to something is good, like having a reaction to medication versus responding to the medication. In transitioning to the ICU system, you can dramatically reduce the reactions while increasing positive responses by leading teachers into the necessary paradigm shift.

Besides the Tear Down section of this book, plenty of information is available to show how badly the zero system stinks, and there is strong research to support the "Power of I." When a portion of the Tear Down information was presented recently to a middle school staff, one teacher broke down and started crying. She explained later, "I came in here totally against changing to this crazy no zero thing, but after listening and really thinking about it, it made me cry. I realized the things we have been doing really do hurt some students. I am sold out now and will give all of my efforts to building a new system based on never giving a zero or accepting low quality work again." Her school is off and running using the ICU system to communicate missing assignments and they are reporting very positive changes in student attitudes.

It's not about you

Principals that think the school revolves around them cannot implement this new plan because it relies heavily on allowing teachers to solve problems and grow professionally. A new system is being developed, and teachers will rebel if principals do not meet frequently and listen to the teachers. If you love having the best parking space and being "the boss," don't even give this a shot because you are stuck on yourself instead of your students. If your heart is right, give your teachers time to learn as much as possible about the No Zero approach and the ICU system by exposing them to plenty of easy to read research. This will break the ice and get them thinking. Include enough evidence on the weakness in the present zero system to make them want to try something else.

Core Team

Develop a small team or two teams to visit schools, study in depth with you, and totally buy into the new mindset. "Cultural Inconsistencies" and "Quit Fooling Yourselves" point out major flaws, and your Core Team should be very familiar with these sections. Some teachers will flip-flop on you during the transition by appearing to agree one day only to change back after eating lunch with some naysayers. Your Core Team must be saturated with information and be trusted to not change directions when things get messy.

These teachers will be your bridge when you cross over to the "I." They must be allowed to problem solve with you from the very beginning. Do not dominate the meetings; instead, facilitate. Many schools have transitioned successfully by discussing research, developing a core team, and preparing the entire staff for approximately one semester. January is not a bad time to start the process because it gives you the summer to attend the Southern Region Education Board annual conference and get everybody on board. Although the principal must be patient, a stubbornness and commitment to change is essential. Otherwise, as soon as the first complaints start coming in, cowering down and backing off will doom the necessary changes.

Administrators United

Make sure your assistant principals are equally committed, informed, and involved. Teachers will follow the administration's lead if they sense a unified front. Changing the role of classified and some certified personnel is essential. The success of the new grading system has to be the top priority. Everything from class schedules to pep rallies need to be revisited constantly. Provide as many "Lifeguards" (explained later) as you possibly can and keep looking for more adults to support the teachers. You must sell the teachers on the importance of drastically increasing parent contacts and then find a simple way to place contact information at teachers' fingertips. Require one parent contact per day and hold the teachers to it, otherwise expect no change in their habits. Check the ICU list every time a student is in your office. It will only take a minute and it helps to change the student paradigm quickly. No matter how large your school is, if all administrators are united, the school can be divided to make the system manageable. Administrators should make some phone calls about missing assignments to stay directly involved and show teachers this will be a team effort. Wise principals will take the highest maintenance students on as their own projects. Being personally involved in transforming some of these students will help to quickly improve your school culture and motivate the rest of your staff.

Small Groups & Short Meetings

Reduce the number of faculty meetings the first two years and increase the number of small group meetings. Meeting during their planning times at least once a month will reduce teacher meltdowns and allow them to give you ideas to problem solve. Ask the same question at every meeting, "What is your number one problem right now?" Someone in the group already has the best solution and your job is to pull everyone together. End every meeting with an open ended, "Let's all try this for a while and we will see if this helps. If you come up with something better, be sure to share it with all of us." Teachers are amazing problem solvers when they think their ideas will be respected.

You will have lots of success stories like the ones mentioned in this book, and it is critical to share these in addition to discussing problems. By sharing success stories, teachers will realize the system is working and be motivated to solve problems instead of complain. When the principal decides they will take on the toughest students, it dramatically increases the system's chance for success. Do not allow any student to get by no matter how stubborn they may seem. Once you develop a successful plan for the toughest character, you will have it whipped and never look back.

ICU Notes

10

HOW THE **ICU** SYSTEM WORKS

The nuts and bolts

"Oh no, another lazy one!" used to be the way we thought when looking at a new student like Josh. He was overweight, moved slowly, showed little emotion, and apathy defined everything about him. His body language screamed, "Getting work out of me is going to be like pulling teeth!" Our teachers, however, had gained a tremendous amount of confidence in our ICU system. The new learning culture he was entering was different and teachers now believed the system would get him going without draining their batteries. ICU stands for Intensive Care Unit just like in a hospital. If you are physically sick enough to be in intensive care, nurses and doctors will do everything within their power to get you back to being able to independently care for your self. We chose ICU because it implies that if a student's grade is sick, we will do everything we can to get them back to being a responsible, independent worker and learner.

Can you feel the cultural contrast between the traditional Zero system and the ICU approach? We know the difference is huge. The traditional zero system continues to kill students like Josh while the ICU system brings them back to life. "Josh, you have got to start coming to school," and "Josh, you have got to turn your work in on time or you will fail," were two of the many useless phrases of encouragement we always tried before ICU.

Linda Crutcher, our amazing guidance counselor, called his former school to help us profile what his problems were. She was told emphatically, "He will not come to school, and if he does he will not lift a finger." Instead of being discouraged, she couldn't wait to see the culture of the ICU system nurse him back to health. Josh arrived in September and within a month or two of doing our thing I sort of forgot about him because I rarely heard his name mentioned. In February, my secretary informed me of a phone call on line one, from Josh. It was around 7:30 and our school day had just started when I picked up and heard an enthusiastic boy blurt out: "I missed the bus and my dad's truck won't start, could you please come get me? I don't want to miss school today!"

This was no small victory; this was evidence that the new culture was working.

ICU Path to Success

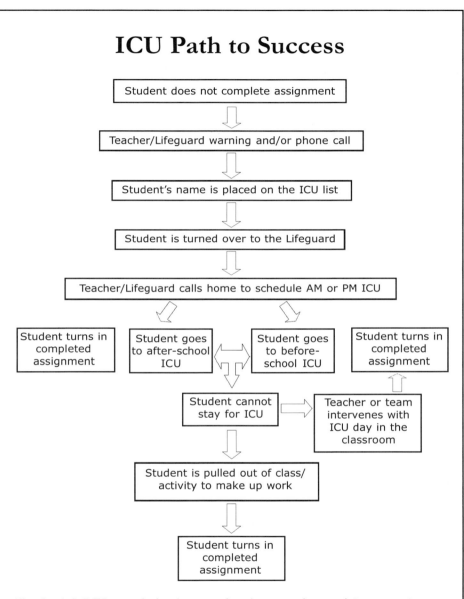

All paths of the ICU system lead to the same end result: every student completing every assignment. The key component of the plan is to provide support at every step of the way, from teachers and lifeguards to before-school and after-school help. After this pathway becomes a part of each student's paradigm, teachers can begin to raise expectations even further.

I emailed all of his teachers and asked for grades and a report on how he was doing. Josh was doing his work on time, making mostly B's with a few A's, and was a pleasure to have in class. Can you see why we laugh when the high school teachers criticize our system? We handed him off to them with excellent study habits and, more importantly, HOPE!

ICU is a communication spreadsheet program for missing assignments that can be viewed by anyone in the building using some form of an intrashare network. Instead of giving speeches, arguing, and wasting time and energy on students who do not have their work, the teacher simply plugs the information into the ICU system. All students know what the ICU list is, and over a short period of time, they do not want to be on it. A single missing assignment becomes a big deal. A single missing assignment means their grade is sick and in need of attention before it becomes fatal. We would never harass, threaten, or chew on someone who was physically in Intensive Care, and we take the exact same approach with their grade. Josh entered our school and within days the teachers treated his apathy differently than his teachers had treated it before, and his fellow students informed him repeatedly: "You might as well do your work, Josh, it just isn't worth fighting anymore!"

Even though every school can afford this system—it costs nothing—only some schools are able to do it. The system is totally dependent on one main ingredient: teachers working together. Our teachers are 100% committed to the new system and they work as a united group to make it better every year. The students hear the exact same thing in every class when they do not turn in an assignment: "Well, I guess I will have to put you on ICU." Josh's story is repeated weekly at our school and other schools who have implemented the system.

Student	Homeroom	English	Math	Social Studies	Science
Joslin	Mr. White	Lesson 12, #1-14			
Jenna	Mrs. Jones		p. 124, 1-19 odd		Life cycle diagram
Zach	Mrs. Smith		p. 124, 1019 odd; Ratio flip chart		
Lauren	Mr. White	Descriptive Essay			
Sam	Ms. Martin			Capitals map	

The beauty of the ICU list is that it doesn't require a special subscription or costly computer software. On its most basic level, it's just a spreadsheet. What makes it useful is sharing the spreadsheet over a school Intrashare network or through a free online hosting site like Google Documents. Visit www.poweroficu.com for more details on how to set up your own shared ICU list or to download template of forms seen in this book.

Everywhere I go, people ask "What about the, you know, really apathetic student that nothing seems to work with, what do you do with them?" Josh was the king of apathy, and that's why we love the ICU communication system.

In building your own system, we put leadership first because without it, the system will fail. However, everything hinges on communication and ICU is just one simple and inexpensive tool everyone can use. Any new system must be built on some type of grading system that refuses to give zeroes or major reform will never take place. As you read the rest of the book, don't forget about Josh. If you want to argue with an idea that we suggest, don't forget that we have proof on our side. At schools using the ICU, children with sick grades eventually get up and walk on their own.

ICU Notes

11

If I don't grade it, they won't do it!

Finding intrinsic motivations for students to complete their work

How many grades do you generally have for a student during a grading period? In asking numerous teachers this question, it is interesting to hear the wide range of answers. This question is significant to ask yourself and discuss as a staff in building up your new ICU system. Why? What does this have to do with giving Incompletes and communicating missing assignments? Many teachers believe that if they don't grade it, the students won't do it. The entire staff needs to trash this paradigm because it's just not true! Did you know that grades and report cards did not even exist in the early schools? Did you know the compulsory attendance laws in the early twentieth century bombarded our teachers with so many students that they came up with grades and report cards out of panic? Did you know that grading and reporting do not enhance education and have never been a necessary ingredient in the learning process? This information will free you from some of the bondage to grades and will lead to a natural improvement in the quality of the assignments you give each day.

Ditto

Ditto was the nickname of a character in a popular old movie, *Teachers*, starring Nick Nolte. The students called the teacher "Ditto" because everyday as they entered his classroom they picked up four ditto sheets to individually work on during the period with no talking allowed. The teacher, Ditto, sat quietly at his desk behind tall stacks of ditto sheets as students picked them up at the beginning and turned them in at the end with no dialogue necessary—this was the accepted routine. One of the funniest parts of the movie was when a student asked to go to the bathroom around 1:30 in the afternoon and Ditto didn't respond. It was later determined by the paramedics that he had actually died around 9:00 in the morning but nobody noticed because he had made himself such an insignificant part of the class.

The old ditto machines are extinct, but in many classrooms the spirit of the ditto sheet lives on. Teachers have bad days like everybody else and the students still show up for class and a lesson is supposed to be taught. Pulling out the crossword puzzles, word searches, and lengthy, boring worksheets (no longer called dittos) to keep them busy because of a sore throat is almost a necessity sometimes. However, these types of assignments must never appear on the ICU list. The ICU list will become like a sacred document the more everyone gets comfortable with it. The culture the ICU system creates is sort of like healthy adult peer pressure where teachers expect each other to cut out the silly assignments.

The process begins with a teacher placing a missing assignment onto the shared ICU list. Let's stop there for a moment. If the principal and staff have done their jobs correctly, a network of adults now have access to and will help run down the single assignment. Teachers who have used ICU for years will tell you, "Do not put any crossword puzzles, word searches, or other dumb, busy work assignments on ICU or you will be embarrassed." Why? Because all the eyes watching and helping are trained adults, not helpless students. This is actually a very healthy result of using the ICU system. As Toni Eubanks says in her workshop, "There is no content standard that requires the students to find the word 'molecule' backwards or diagonally." Teachers know deep down that these assignments are not really important. Even though they will still use them, crosswords will never again receive the high priority some teachers have inappropriately placed on them in the past. More importantly, think about the helpless students getting chewed out, receiving a low grade, or even a zero over a word search not completed in the past.

Formative Assessment Takes Off

Formative assessment strategies discover what your students know and what they don't know to help direct your next instructional decision.

After observing an excellent lesson on singular and plural in a first grade classroom, it appeared all of the students learned what they were supposed to. I wanted to see for sure who learned it and who might be faking it so they would not be embarrassed. "Students put your heads down and close your eyes, no peeking. 'My dog is barking.' In this sentence if you think the word dog is singular, raise your hand. Now, if you think the word dog is plural, raise your hand. Now, if you are not sure, raise your hand. It is okay if you are not sure, I am just doing this to find out for sure if you learned the difference between singular and plural." After giving

---

Teacher Talk

"I never drop the lowest grade anymore. I no longer give participation grades to help buffer low test grades. In my class, student grades are a much better reflection of what they have learned than in years past. We talk to our students a lot more about Learning."

— *Marilyn has been a successful middle school Social Studies teacher for 37 years and continues to improve the quality of her teaching each year.*

"One of the primary tasks of teachers is to design work for students—work that students will find engaging and that will result in their learning that which is valued by the school system, by parents, and by the community at large."
—Schlechty Center for Leadership in School Reform

them five sentences and repeating myself, the teacher and I realized several students still did not have a clue and she decided to spend more time on this standard the next day. This is formative assessment in it purest form because we eliminated any outside help.

Formative assessment strategies give teachers information for student learning. The singular/plural example shows the teacher and students how much they have learned on an individual level. More importantly, it gives teachers information about what they need to do next. Flying through the curriculum because we are afraid we won't cover everything in time for the state achievement test is driving too many of our daily decisions in the classroom.

One of the best by-products of the ICU system is that it will lead teachers to a significant increase in checking for understanding. By having to place every missing assignment on a list everyday, teachers will be naturally drawn to stop grading every little thing. This is a good thing.

Emphasizing learning over doing your work and making good grades will be one of the most significant—but difficult—changes in your daily habits. The reason it will be difficult is totally related to changing what you say every day. How many times during a lesson do you say the word "learn" and how many times during a lesson do you mention "doing work" and "making grades"? Make it a point of professional growth to listen to what you are emphasizing everyday. The end result will be a natural improvement in teaching habits, more student engagement, and an increase in student success. The ICU list must become a list of missing *Quality* assignments that truly represent the standards they are learning.

A poor-quality assignment can be easily changed into a formative assessment tool. Take a pop quiz, for example. Did you give it to get a grade in the box or to check for understanding? Did you take the time necessary after the quiz to allow students to clearly see what they have learned and what they have not learned? Improve the quality of the assignment even more by coaching the students on what they can do to increase their learning. Your students should be soaked in formative assessment and daily hear you say, "Let's find out what you have learned so far."

Taking a grade on an assignment is supposed to be an assessment of learning, summative assessment. Take a very good look at the grades you are giving students. Do each of them reflect student learning? What if you only end up with 5 or 6 grades at the end of a grading period? Is there a magic number? Think *quality* grades over *quantity*. Many of the teachers who give 12-20 grades in a grading period say things like, "I give lots of grades to give them a better chance of passing," or "I give some easy grades to help buffer the low test grades." This is a poor habit we all developed with the weak, dead end, zero system.

Under the new ICU system, students are given a chance to redo work and eventually (hopefully) restudy material and retake tests. Students learning the material is the total emphasis now and they have more freedom and opportunity to accomplish this. In other words, cut out all of the padded and rinky-dink grades you have been including in your grading system because they are being replaced with much better quality grades. If you're afraid this won't prepare them for college, think back to your college days. I cannot remember any college professor who took more than a handful of grades for the entire course. Grading or scoring a test, project, or assignment should only be done after a healthy amount of instruction has taken place. A good rule of thumb is if a significant number of students score poorly on a test, project, or assignment, then more formative assessment opportunities/activities are needed. Give quality assignments and stop feeling pressure to get a lot of grades in those little boxes in the grade book!

ICU Notes

$$\boxed{12}$$

SEAMLESS COMMUNICATION

The importance of staying in touch

Students are winning

Imagine being a head coach of a high school football team. The first half of the game was a disaster because the other team had a running back who was beating you single-handedly. Where do you begin in sorting out the number one goal for the second half? Obviously, every good coach will say, "Take away what they do best" or "Take away what they like to do the most." So, in the second half, you put all eleven players on the line of scrimmage and dare the quarterback to throw the ball. Even if you lose, you at least made them change what they were doing. Apathetic students have the upper hand; they are in control and they know it. Be a good coach and take away what they are doing because they are winning.

Let's look at the three best arguments apathetic students rely on to avoid doing assignments:

"I didn't know I owed you anything" — Implies the teacher did not tell them.

"I thought I already turned that in" — Implies the teacher lost it.

"I didn't understand, you didn't explain it" — Implies the teacher does not explain things clearly.

The magic in these three responses can be deceiving. Teachers are sucked into a mini-debate daily and they actually convince themselves they win when the conversation is over because they are the teacher and they hold the ultimate power of giving the grade.

The implications put teachers on the defensive. "I told you three times," or "It is written right there on my board" slams the first argument. And of course, does "I do not have it, so you did NOT turn it in" take care of their second argument? No it doesn't! "I clearly explained the assignment several times" and "Why do all these other students have theirs if I didn't explain it" is a waste of energy. They say it, parents believe it, and they win every time. Admit it: if they don't care about a low

Student	Contact Method	Date	Time	Name of Contact	Phone #	Notes
Joslin	Phone	2/2/09	9:45 am	Cynthia (mother)	123-4567	Arranged a.m. ICU
Jenna	Email	2/9/09	3:30 pm	Robert (father)	123-4567	Requested conference
Zach	Meeting	1/26/09	11:30 am	George and Jessica (parents)	123-4567	Discussed problems with work completion/death in the family
Lauren	Letter	2/13/09	1 pm	Parents	123-4567	Requested conference/missing assignments
Sam	Meeting	3/16/09	2 pm	Grandmother	123-4567	Arranged p.m. ICU 3/19/09

Althought contact logs are nothing new, by creating the contact log as a shared document, one that can be viewed and edited by any teacher in the building, its power as a communication tool is magnified. For more information on setting up a shared contact log—as well as to download a contact log template—visit www.poweroficu.com.

grade, they win! In fact, the student has built an army of support behind them. The parents stand behind their babies because they remember a teacher doing that to them when they were in school. When the student's friends spend the night they join in agreement with, "Mrs. Hubbell loses my stuff all the time, too!" While at church or at the grocery store the friend's parents unite with, "We are having the same problem with Mrs. Hubbell, evidently she just doesn't know how to explain things to our sweeties."

Look clearly at this very true picture of what actually happens when a student doesn't turn in an assignment. It is not just a one-on-one, teacher vs. student, with the teacher holding the upper hand. Instead, it is teacher vs. student and the small army of supporters they have recruited and work hard to maintain.

Shift the parents

Shifting the parents is unbelievably easy and is well worth the time and effort. Placing the missing assignment on the ICU list and keeping the list updated leaves the students helpless. Remember, the ICU list is out there for all adults in the building to see and support. By dropping the zero and all the threats that go with it, teachers and parents will join hands quickly because both agree assignments should be completed. It is this "disarming" of the students that is the coolest part for teachers to experience. Students have been in control for years and are left standing alone with nobody to blame. Even their friends abandon their little army of support because they have a new battle of their own to fight: their parents. One of our teachers was trying to explain this to a group of visiting teachers recently. She said, "The students eventually just kind of go…well…limp is the best word for it, and then they start doing their work."

Look back at the three best arguments mentioned above and then imagine a tool that is at everyone's fingertips that shows exactly what is owed and by whom. These student comebacks can and will become extinct, useless, a memory, after effectively implementing the ICU communication system. Effectively implementing this means all administrators, counselors, advisory teachers, coaches, band directors, choir directors, drama coaches and even club sponsors dealing with students can simply click on the ICU list and hold their students accountable. Checking on grades every three weeks for your players or club members is replaced by daily checking of the ICU list. When coaches give out consequences for missing a single assignment, players will be begging their teachers not to put them on the list.

Communicate like crazy what every student owes and become an army of support for each other. We are *replacing* time and energy we already spend with new habits that will save time, energy, and especially teacher frustration in the long run. Habits take time and this one will be more than worth the effort. Within a few months of all staff members making the ICU list a routine, students will completely stop using their old arguments.

To Be Perfectly Clear

Building a communication system to daily broadcast missing assignments will strip students of their power as long as the grading system is based on "Incompletes" rather than allowing zero as an option.

Legion of support

Students know they are fighting a losing battle and finally start doing their assignments when they see the "Legion of Support" the teacher has behind him or her.

—**Parents** have shifted and have stopped listening to their excuses

—**Coaches** discipline for missing work

—**Lifeguards** are certified or classified staff member assigned to assist teachers. They will hound students over any missing assignment and offer extra time options.

—**Advisory teachers** mention missing assignments first thing in the morning

—The **drama coach, choir director**, and **band director** check ICU routinely

—The **principal, guidance counselor**, and **other staff members** will also check the ICU often, talk to students at-risk of needing Intensive Care, and find solutions to keep everyone's assignments in good health.

Communicate like crazy

Don't stop with just the ICU list. Instead, keep pouring on the communication of missing work with multiple tools.

Teachers should have a permanent small section of their board for work not completed. Divide the section up for each period of the day. Instead of giving the old, useless speeches when a student doesn't have their work, simply tell them to write their name in the proper section of the board. When the work is turned in and you accept it as quality work they can erase their name. This becomes a habit within two to three weeks. Teachers really enjoy not wasting time, energy, and raising their blood pressure by simply plugging the student into the system.

E-mail parents right in front of the student. This is another great tool and it can become a habit. Once again it is a habit change because teachers must collect parent e-mails and put them in their address book. Do teachers need to use this with every assignment owed with every student? Of course not, but it is so unbelievably effective with certain students that teachers will crave this one after using it a few times.

Call parents during planning time. If teachers would just call one parent a day, or an average of five parents per week, this tool will help change student habits. The phone calls go smoothly because parents are no longer hearing, "Your son/daughter already has three zeroes and they are doing nothing in my class." Instead, parents hear a teacher simply letting them know their child owes the assignment and they are very appreciative.

The best schools will develop a way for teachers to record parent contacts. Advisory teachers being responsible for updating the contact information on their 20-25 students is not difficult. Placing all of the student contact information on some sort of shared document places email addresses and phone numbers at teacher's fingertips.

Students get lost in middle school and high school. If you needed to contact Jenna's parents because she had a missing assignment, a Parent Contact Log might show that Mr. Luckett called Jenna's mom last week. One of the parent's favorite arguments, "You are the only teacher who seems to be having a problem with little

Teacher Talk

"For years, we as teachers and administrators have been communicating and monitoring attendance and discipline school-wide on a daily basis. Why have we not been doing this with the most important issue, students' academic assignments. Please move your energy toward the assignments, because the assignments are the only one that truly measure what is being learned by the student."

—Middle School Principal

Jenna" is blown out of the water when the contact log shows two other teachers have called recently with the same problem. If every teacher will make just one parent phone call per day and send out emails routinely, parents will begin to appreciate and trust the teachers. This places an enormous amount of pressure on the students and apathy begins to melt away. If only a handful of teachers make use of this practice, don't expect drastic results.

This is a great time to refer back to the section on Paradigm Paralysis. If you find yourself thinking under the old paradigm, the section you just read on communication may seem either impractical or like too much work. If this happens, remember the statement "when data falls outside our paradigm, we find it hard to see and accept." Do not let your thinking freeze up. The hardest thing about trying to explain the ICU system is that teachers cannot "see" and "accept" that their student paradigm will change and their habits will improve. Be tenacious, stick together, and stubbornly problem solve through each issue. Students have been pounded with all of our attempts to make the zero system work, so they need time to respond to the new paradigm. The ICU system will work and students will change.

THE STUDENT ARMY WITHOUT THE ICU

PHASE 1:
In this situation,
the Students
are winning

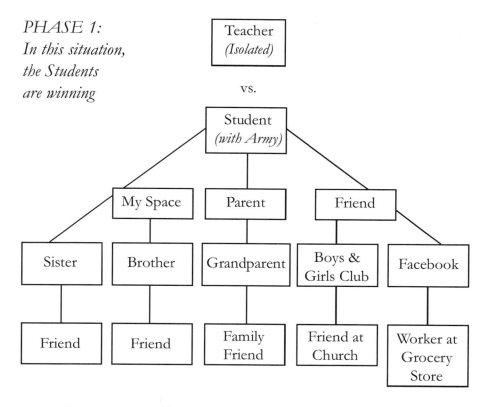

The student builds an Army of Support for their cause that tears away at any credibility the teacher has, making us all question if the teacher is correct.

The ICU will DESTROY the Student Army

The Teacher Army WITH the ICU

PHASE 2:
In this situation,
the Teachers
are winning

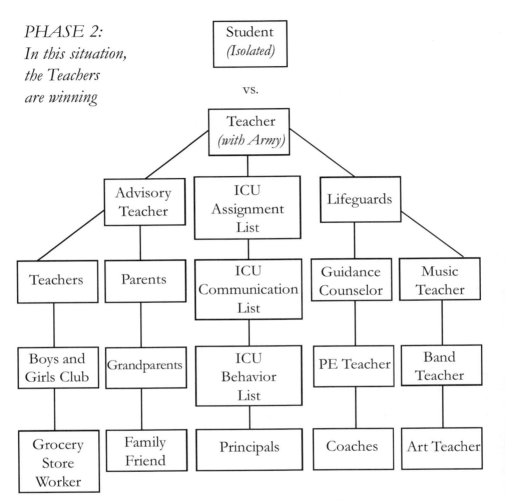

The Teacher builds an Army of Support that tears away at any credibility the apathetic student has, and ultimately the student is left standing alone.

The ICU will BUILD the Student Army

THE TEACHER & STUDENT ARMY WITH THE ICU

PHASE 3:
No one left
to fight

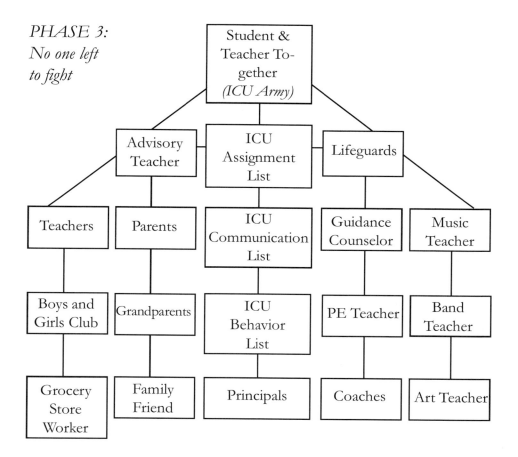

The student is tired of being alone and joins teams with the teacher.
The teacher and student then build an Army of Support together
that creates success and accountability for all involved.

The ICU Army WINS!

ICU Notes

13

SPEAK A DIFFERENT LANGUAGE

What you say and how you say it can make a world of difference

William Glasser, in his book *Every Student Can Succeed*, lists deadly habits teachers routinely use to try to control their students. He uses the term "deadly habits" because they just do not work. The list includes criticizing, blaming, complaining, nagging, threatening, punishing, and rewarding. The language teachers choose to use on a daily basis is more important than teachers realize. If Glasser is correct, then teachers should get excited about a fresh language that really works. We suggest teachers:

Completely stop making statements using If/then. "If you don't _____ (do your work, get your work in on time, give it to me tomorrow etc.), then you will _____ (lose 50 points, get an F, etc.)." Just think of all the wasteful threats we fill in the blanks with. Save your energy for the productive ICU system.

Stop giving speeches about how irresponsible they are and how they will not be ready for _____ (the next grade, college, real world, etc.). Nagging students with these speeches makes you look bad because students have grown immune to them and actually have pretty good comebacks. Several students have a parent, uncle, or friend who dropped out and make a lot more money than we do. Save your energy for the ICU system.

Stop complaining/blaming students for poor quality work or not turning in assignments because it is a total waste of time and energy. Just stop it if you can. How many times have you said to your apathetic students, "I care more about you succeeding than you do"? Besides not saying this anymore, you must stop thinking it. Use all of this wasted energy to help solve the new issues you and your colleagues will face with the ICU system. Apathetic students will become isolated by the system and there will be no need to fuss at them.

"Tiny differences can make huge differences in life. When a guy calls a girl a kitten, she'll love him; if he calls her a cat, he'll have a serious problem. Tell her she's a vision and she'll smile all over, but call her a sight and you won't get invited back. You can take tiny steps and score small points—but they all add up."

—Zig Ziglar

Stop getting angry and taking it personally when poor quality work or no work at all is turned in. Many teachers take it personally when assignments are not completed. The defensive language towards the student often damages their relationship and ultimately has a negative effect on learning. Getting angry uses up a lot of energy and this energy will be needed to build the ICU system which actually works. Many teachers have convinced themselves they have only two choices in dealing with apathetic students: really care about their students, which means nagging, getting angry, fussing, and giving speeches; or, stop caring about them and just turn cold towards them so they will stop "wasting their time." ICU offers a true option: Care enough about them to spend positive time and energy to help build the ICU system because it will really make a difference.

Stop mixing student behavior issues with academic issues. Teachers waste a lot of time and energy trying to "get back at" disrespectful or disruptive students by using a bad grade as a weapon. How do teachers do this? They say they don't grade behaviors, but when the class is misbehaving and the teacher gives a pop quiz or makes everyone write a paragraph, a page, or a report—that often doesn't even reflect the true skills students need—that is exactly what's happening. This wears the teacher out and most of the time the student doesn't really care. More importantly, it is unprofessional to punish bad behavior with a low grade. Consistent consequences for poor behavior is essential, but should be dealt with as a separate issue. All of your energy is needed to build and keep improving the ICU system which will give real authority back to the teachers and drastically reduce student apathy. The schools using the ICU system report dramatic declines in behavior problems because the students who used to act out are now engaged in their school work. Keep grades and behavior separate!

Stop rewarding students constantly for doing things they are expected or required to do. Some rewards are a great idea because of the positive culture they may help develop. However, giving rewards for turning in work on time is a bad idea and a waste of your time and energy. Quarterly rewards for all students who have never been on the ICU list is not a bad idea, if it can be done in a simple and inexpensive manner.

Remember, the ICU grading system does not give points for bringing in canned goods, returning report cards on time, or cleaning the teacher's board. One of my former students gave me that last one. She said her high school Spanish teacher gave her twenty bonus points last week for cleaning her board. She added, "The only way I am going to pass Spanish is if she lets me clean her board several more times." Is this the kind of skill that high school teachers worry about kids missing out on by being "enabled" by No Zero grading policies? We must cut out this nonsense and teach students to learn the material and reward them by giving them grades that reflect true learning.

Four Powerful Questions!

Who do you owe? Students will no longer lie because they know their missing assignments are broadcast school-wide. All day long, any teacher, principal, counselor, coach, or other caring adult can stop any student for a one minute conversation started with this question.

What do you owe? In the past, students would not have had a clue what they owed, but all of them will know exactly what they owe now. Students being able to tell you what they owe, leads naturally to the next question.

What do you need? Do you need extra time? Do you need extra help? Do you need a pencil, paper, graph paper, colored pencils, or poster board? Believe it or not, students generally say they do not need any supplies. They will usually ask for extra help in math only. However, several students will ask for extra time. Dr. Bottoms, the executive vice president of the SREB, is correct, or at least very close to being right, when he claims that all students will do every assignment if given enough of one thing-TIME!

How can I help you? If you were a struggling student, how would it make you feel if you were asked this question several times throughout the day instead of being chewed out?

Judge or Advocate

If every adult in your school would completely stop using the deadly habits of language and replace them with these four questions routinely, the culture of your school would change overnight! Many schools are viewed as an adversarial environment in which teachers are in complete control, students must conform, and parents do not feel welcome. The bottom line is the community no longer trusts their schools and the schools no longer trust the community. These schools are generally dominated by teachers who view themselves as judges. Their job is to judge the students' performance and then tell the parents thumbs up or thumbs down about their child.

Schools dominated by teachers who view themselves as advocates for the students have a totally different feel. These student advocates naturally speak a different language and wish all of their colleagues would. Speaking a different language sends a completely different message to everyone and is a key component in building a bridge of trust. One of the reasons we say the "Power"of the ICU is because its' ripple effects bring about powerful culture changes and the community will begin talking positively about your school.

Changing your language can and should bring you back to your original love for teaching. You will be amazed at how your toughest students will talk with you about education. Students will be in shock the first few times these questions are asked,

Teacher Talk

"I had been out for two days due to my daughter's illness. One of the assignments I left with the substitute was for my science class to write a short essay explaining the Water Cycle. They were instructed to include all of the phases. They blew it off as busy work. The quality of the essays was very poor. Instead of the old speeches and the threats of low grades, I told them I was thinking about taking them on a field trip to McDonald's. I hope all of you order a hamburger, fries, and a drink and then they leave the fries out of the order. "But if we ordered fries we should get our fries!" they argued. "Not necessarily," I added, "if these essays were my lunch order, most of you left out the fries. In fact, some of you left out the drink also. An assignment is like an order at a restaurant, I expect you to all give me what I order."

—Janie said her students responded with excellent essays after this short but effective correlation to a real life explanation. She has been an effective teacher for seven years, but is experiencing daily improvements in the language she uses with her students.

> In the past, schools were apparently organized around the belief that students are motivated by the **fear of failure**; we now recognize that such a belief only reinforces an already poor self-concept. ***Fear of failure can only motivate students who have a pattern of success.***
>
> — *"Success Breeds Success," Charlotte Danielson*

but over time the questions will become commonplace among all stakeholders in your school. Anyone can ask these questions, from front office personnel to teachers to custodians. These four questions can become a way of life for your school and no student will be able to escape from them. The questions are not harmful, they are not shameful, and in no way are they hard to answer. These questions are possibly the most powerful accountability tool you will inherit.

Administrators should take the lead by being consistent and finding the right students to ask each day. Remember, if you want this to work, then you should work with some of the toughest students to reach. First thing every morning, administrators and counselors should try to call a few students to the office. Ask each student what and who they owe. After they tell you, double check with the ICU list inviting them to look on your computer with you. You will find yourself starting everyday with a purpose and a true look into the eyes of your students. If you say students are important to you, then put your words to task and begin everyday by checking on your students and help them create a plan of attack. Ask the four questions and then have the Power of "ICU" system behind the questions and you will become an empowered teaching staff that moves from "We are teachers" to "We are instructional leaders." Although you may think these questions will lead to an enabling culture, do not predict what you have not tried. The ICU system builds responsibility if everyone gets on board and continues to require all assignments be completed. Are you thinking students will wait forever to turn things in? Actually, just the opposite is true. If every teacher refuses to give in and the communication network is consistently followed, assignments will be turned in ON TIME! Believe it.

Stop the Madness associated with the "deadly habits" and ask these four most powerful questions. Watch what happens.

ICU Notes

THE TEACHER

The greatest responsibility

The teacher is the most important person in any school. A great principal with poor teachers makes for a weak school. However, a school with great teachers is a great school even if the principal is weak. Parents and students are only concerned with the attitude and heart of the teacher. Knowledge of their subject, of course is significant as long as the teacher doesn't buy into the poisonous, "I'm here to teach math, if they want it they can get it, if not, fine." Outstanding teachers will have no problem adjusting to giving incompletes, communicating missing assignments, and changing their habits. The reason they won't have a problem is because their hearts are centered on students. Loving students is the highest standard a teacher, principal, or school can have. How can we have high expectations for our students but allow low expectations from the teachers?

So what is the problem with teachers shifting to the new system? All teachers are not centered on students. Just ask the students and they will tell you without hesitation which teachers care about them. Have you ever heard the saying, "Students don't care how much you know until they know how much you care"? Our guidance counselor, Linda, is a new-teacher mentor and drills this into the paradigm of every new teacher. At least two times per year, we spend quality time in faculty meetings discussing the importance of this concept being the backbone of everything we do. Write it on your desk and remind yourself of this at the beginning of every day.

Listening to the knee jerk reaction from many teachers to the new system before even giving it a try is powerful evidence that too many teachers have forgotten why they entered the profession. "What about my deadline?" sounds like a spoiled child who thinks the world revolves around them.

To simplify the teacher's changing role in the new system, begin with not allowing weak, negative, and whiny teachers to fake it by continuing with the old zero system while giving lip service to the administration. I spoke in a small county recently where the director of schools was trying to move his system away from zeroes. Although, the middle school was having lots of success, the high school

> *"Outstanding educators know that*
> *if a school has great teachers,*
> *it is a great school.*
> *There are two ways to improve a school*
> *significantly:*
> *get better teachers and*
> *improve the teachers in the school."*
> —**Todd Whitaker**

principal was allowing teachers to fake it. During the break in my presentation, several of the high school teachers told me they wanted to change, but the principal was allowing high school teachers to put 5's and 10's in the grade boxes, thus following the directors wish to stop giving zeroes.

Toni Eubanks reports that in some of the schools she has worked with, teachers have found a more troubling way to "fake it." In many situations, there were teachers who were opposed to the idea of giving students extra chances to do their work, but they were also worried about being confronted by their principals with the dreaded "grade analysis report," a report that would show that many of their students had actually gotten Ds and Fs for the quarter or semester. To beat the system, they wouldn't "waste their time" by chasing down assignments or having students re-do work or re-take tests. They would simply grade the work and give the students back the grade they earned, but then record a grade of 70, the lowest passing score in the district, into the grade book. This way, no students actually failed, and no one brought it to the principal's attention because there were no complaining parents or students. Eubanks learned of this practice through these teachers' colleagues, who were caring, professional, hard-working teachers who were so appalled by their colleagues' behaviors that they felt compelled to share the practice with her.

Next, teachers need to put lots of energy into the ICU list even though it will be uncomfortable at first. There are enough teachers using this now to testify to how easy and valuable it is once you get used to it. Believe in the significance of broadcasting missing assignments by keeping the ICU list accurate. By forcing yourself to list missing assignments, you will naturally want to reduce the large number of assignments you are grading unnecessarily.

Question the quality of every assignment you are expecting students to turn in. Develop a healthy habit of contacting parents. We underestimate middle and high school parents by thinking they really don't care. The best secondary teachers do contact their students' parents and these teachers lose very few of their students to failure. Teachers: believe it, test it, and make it a new habit. We overestimate secondary students when we think, "They are old enough to …" This is ridiculous and a cop out. Don't we have high school students that still act like elementary students? All students mature at different times and involving the parents in the daily missing assignments will reap major dividends.

Finally, grow into an instructional leader by becoming a problem solver. The infant stage of changing systems is fragile and will only grow if enough teachers look for answers rather than pointing out the problems. The administration must follow up with the network of adults to support the list and develop individual plans for extra time and extra help. If this is handled properly by your administrator, it will help you relax and trust the system. Be straightforward with your principal if they are not listening to your solutions.

We now save lots of energy and our stress level is significantly lower because every teacher trusts the system. After several years of using the ICU system, Mike Presley, our Algebra 1 teacher, had a student tell him recently she did not have her homework. He said the room got very quiet because it had been so long since he and the class had heard anyone say this. Did he get the work? Of course. Did it drain his energy? Absolutely not. In fact, the girl had her assignment doubled and it was turned in the very next day. Given enough time, this really works and you will be getting a much higher percentage of assignments turned in on time.

The Power of ICU is an intrinsic program based on building professionalism, intrinsic desire, and a seamless form of communication.

Teacher Talk

"I had taught for several years in a different state and really struggled with this at first. Now, I never get mad if a student misses an assignment because we both know it will be completed. I love our system and I enjoy sharing it when people visit, even though I still don't think they believe us sometimes."

—*Lynn, 8th grade Language Arts teacher*

ICU Notes

15

LIFEGUARDS

Lifeguards prevent students from drowning

Lifeguards: A teacher or classified person who works the ICU list everyday. They talk to students, go to lockers, call parents, talk to guidance counselors and administrators, clear up misunderstandings, get to know students, help determine what is needed: extra time, extra help, supplies, organization help, etc., and find solutions for individual problems. The head lifeguard needs to have between one hour and an hour and a half each day assigned to working the ICU list. They can oversee at least 500 students comfortably. This may sound like a lot, but with only about 10 to 15% of students being high maintenance, the number of actual students needing attention is between 50-60. Please remember that this number will keep coming down after the system is in place for a short period of time because student paradigms shift. When paradigms shift, the process really becomes fun. The number of high maintenance students steadily declines.

Part time lifeguards: The more adult eyes that watch the ICU list the better the system will work. Counselors, administrators, advisory teachers, coaches, band directors, choir directors, and club sponsors all should be checking the ICU list frequently. Developing and using the ICU list effectively will not only cure most of your apathetic students, but it is awesome in catching a student who has done well in the past but starts to slip. Coaches make the entire team run if anyone owes work. Band and choir directors have consequences, while club sponsors use their relationships to encourage and help. This works so well it is almost hard to believe any educator would resist getting involved. Think of the conversations that become a habit each day. A student owing one math assignment, for example, could and should be asked, "What's up with the math you owe Mr. Presley?" by three or four adults within the day. The only word to describe the change in students is "amazing."

Parent meetings: Counselors, lifeguards, teachers, and administrators should call a parent meeting anytime a student is either missing an assignment for several days or missing too many assignments. These meetings are usually very beneficial because all the pressure is on the student. All the past arguments like, "If I had only known" or "he/she wasn't aware" have been wiped out by the new system. Parent meetings help tremendously with some students and it is worth the time and effort to fix one student at a time.

Providing lifeguards to watch over missing student work should never replace good habits by the regular classroom teacher. In other words, teachers should not be allowed to dump on the lifeguards. Nothing replaces one-on-one communication between teachers, students, and parents. A bridge of trust is built every time this communication takes place and it contributes greatly to the success of the child. Lifeguards are supplemental to help teachers from getting overwhelmed.

Teachers have been left alone to fight the problem of student apathy for too long. Can you see the army of support the ICU system builds behind individual teachers? If you refuse to implement a No Zero system like ICU, then at least stop saying things like "We are doing everything we can!" or "We've tried EVERY-THING!" when talking about apathetic students. Once again, the biggest barrier you face is trying to build unified support for the program from teachers, staff, and administrators.

Students are in control under the zero system because they can simply refuse to do the work and take a zero. No matter how much teachers care about their students and encourage them, too many students are simply opting out, taking the easiest route, and accepting their own failure. Is it possible for teachers to regain control? With all of the nonsense teachers hear, new programs and ideas forced on them, along with co-worker apathy, it is almost scary to believe things can drastically change. Take away, remove, eliminate, blow up student's tried and true daily responses they feed parents and teachers. The curiosity of what might happen should at least intrigue even the most apathetic teacher.

ICU Notes

16

EXTRA TIME & EXTRA HELP

Two ingredients to eradicate failure

When adults need extra time to finish or redo work, they simply stay late or come in early to finish it. Accountants are a very good example because when quarterly reports are due, they come in early, stay late, and work weekends. Adults are able to stay in their work setting where all of their resources are at their fingertips. This is the same pattern of thought educators should use when setting up opportunities for extra time for their students. Kindergarten teachers, and in most of the lower grades, teachers give students extra time, extra help, never give zeroes, and they are expected to cover a massive number of curriculum standards. Why should teachers in the upper grades have a totally opposite approach to their students?

First of all, the mindset that a student is in trouble or should be ashamed because they need more time must be changed. For another real world example, does the boss argue with and demean the accountant for coming in on the weekend or after hours to complete the task at hand? Most likely, the accountant receives rewards for taking the extra time to complete the task. Educators must buy into the paradigm that many students simply need more time, and then provide it. "If they don't finish it at school, then they can just work on it at home" is the usual battle cry. Don't forget: whatever restrictions we put on our students should apply to adults as well since we are preparing them for the real world. Remaining in the school setting gives students a much better chance for success because many times that is where

Teacher Talk

"I was a vocal opponent of it [the ICU system] at first. I was afraid we were not doing any favors by giving extra time and help. Now I see the focus is more on learning. By putting the emphasis on learning we are better preparing them for college and the real world."
— *Teacher at Southside Elementary*

their resources are, not at home. Finding extra time at school also eliminates the disadvantage many of our students face who have bad situations at home. The premise behind the argument and example of the accountant is that extra time has to be made available to all stakeholders to complete tasks. Due to this shift in thinking, all staff members, every single one, must begin analyzing the school day and finding extra time for students. To look at the school day one must look at the start time, finish time, schedule during the day, what time students arrive and leave on buses, how much time is spent on pep rallies, and any single moment throughout the day where a student can receive extra time and help. Please understand, under the old zero-based system, extra time is a moot point because by the time everyone figures out the work is late, either a zero has been given or so many points have already been deducted that the student has no motivation to do the assignment.

The most effective extra time is after school or on Saturday. For example, If school ends at 2:30, try to set up an after school time of one hour, four days a week. The administrator should try to find funding for this through state money, local money, or fund it through the school. Teachers should be compensated for after-school, before-school, or Saturday extra time if at all possible. As a last resort, teachers may offer to volunteer for one week per semester to make this happen. By using the communication tools discussed earlier, when a child shows up for after school time, there should be no question about what they are to work on. Name the after school-time something like FAILSAFE, RESCUE, HELP, PASS, or simply after-school. Names like "Detention" should be avoided because they have a negative connotation, and you don't want students to have a negative view of a program that exists solely to help them learn.

A late school start time such as 8:00 or later might provide a very good before-school opportunity for extra time. Sometimes buses arrive 30 to 45 minutes before the school day begins, and this is wasted time anyway. Just 30 minutes, two or three times a week, is all some students need to get caught up and stay caught up. If the paradigm of the students has changed and the work they owe is easy to find, students will crave this extra time and teachers will be shocked when they show up on their own.

Sometimes you have to find the time they love best and take it away, being careful to choose language that doesn't berate the students in the process. We are always "offering opportunities" for extra time to complete or re-do assignments, and their schedule during the day is under the school's management to best decide how to help them learn. Extra time works best when it is on the student's time, like before or after school. However, there are times during the school day that may also fit in this category. Choir, band, PE, art, and other favorite times during the day have been used at many schools to allow for extra time. Sometimes a "working lunch" is all a student needs to catch up. Hopefully, these times will only be used occasionally. The students will either get their work in on time or find an after-school or before-school alternative to keep from missing their favorite time. What's amusing is when the students end up asking if they can just do it at home, and many times that is what happens.

Our goal was to do everything within our power to get every child *engaged* in the learning process.

With enough individuals helping, a student ends up with something that special education teachers call an "Individual Education Plan." You will find yourself creating an individualized plan for every student. For example, Kade may stay late every Tuesday and Thursday, Sydney may stay only on Monday afternoons, Andy and Barney may ride the bus so they can come in for an extra thirty minutes before school every day, while Elvis can't come in early or stay late, so he works on school work one day a week instead of going to choir. Eventually, Elvis decides he loves to sing, so he starts doing his work at home. The harder a school staff works to find extra time, the more opportunities can be offered to students.

Just how many subgroups are there for us to monitor for Adequate Yearly Progress? It seems like there are always classifications being added. The next subgroup will probably be "brown-haired girls who like small dogs." This is an exaggeration, of course, but it does hit on an important point. Although trying to meet all the requirements of the No Child Left Behind legislation drives us crazy sometimes, the spirit behind the thinking is to make teachers look at students as individuals. As educators, we often try to fit students into the classifications we are most familiar with or that we were most familiar with when we were in school. These classifications remind us that there are about as many types of students as there are students themselves. We did not develop the ICU system to try to meet the requirements of any federal law or to address poor results from disaggregated test score data. Our goal was to do everything within our power to get every child engaged in the learning process. Looking back, the neatest thing about what we have done is that it taught us a practical way to develop a plan for the specific needs of each student as an individual. When this is done, worries about AYP and NCLB fall away.

Extra Help—What can we do with math?

After working hard to create the ICU system, we found at the end of the third year that the extra time we were providing was taking care of all subjects except one: math. The frustration with this one subject caused us to dig a little deeper into research so we could get ideas from people a lot smarter than ourselves. Based on our experiences, we agree with Dr. William Glasser who states, "math is much more related to innate ability than other subjects. In the end you either know it or you don't. Unlike English or history, effort may not do very much for students who don't have the ability to do math." This quote comes from his excellent book *Every Student Can Succeed.*

The way we word it is, "Not everybody can slam dunk a basketball." Even so, frustrated teachers keep shouting "Jump higher! You're just not trying hard enough!" Meanwhile, schools across the country, especially high schools, have been handed down more math requirements from the guys making all the rules. Evidently, they know more than Dr. Glasser and other researchers who study this everyday.

What can we do about this dilemma? More effort/time helps very little in math. In our experience with the ICU system, over 90% of missing assignments are related to math, and most of our dropouts are related to math.

More math is being required

Over the past two years we have drastically increased extra help opportunities in math for our students in grades 4-8. Our programs from the first year seemed to help, but this year has been great!

Students will soak up extra help if it is given in a way that is comfortable to them. Once again, we are repeating the theme of developing an individual plan. However, instead of getting stressed out about giving an individualized test or standardized assessment in math, we are throwing every kind of extra help we can think of at them, and then they capture what is most comfortable for them.

Have you ever noticed how a good math teacher will always have a student at his or her desk explaining a problem? Before school, during class, after class, during planning time, and after math class, math teachers seem to enjoy talking individual students through tough problems. This process usually involves explaining a concept in a variety of ways, trying to find one that will make sense to the student. One of the great things about the ICU system is that it is not a static program; there is no official end to its development. If something doesn't work in a particular school or classroom, the flexibility is there to fix it. We are still brainstorming and trying everything we can think of to take the effectiveness of the ICU and expand it until we can totally fix our math dilemma.

Our math teachers have been amazed at how effectively they have been able to mentor students to work one-on-one with struggling peers. We have a math help sign up board in our hallway for students to sign up for a forty-five minute session

We are not presenting a theory of what *might* happen *if* you try this. We are watching formerly apathetic students respond dramatically.

to help them learn how to do a difficult problem. The number of times they can come is something we are still developing. The math extra help time is for anyone. We have designed it so there is a teacher who has recruited four peer tutors and all of them are excellent. This has grown into a model for extra help in math, and I say that because of what I see everyday: students consistently helping other students and everyone totally engaged in learning math. Because there is no stigma attached to math extra help—students sign up voluntarily—the program has grown to the point that we need more tutors. By next year, we hope to recruit retirees and college education students to be mentors. Multiply what works.

Although our after school program was started as an extra time intervention, it has naturally changed into extra help in math. If we have 12 students stay after school, at least nine of them will be working on math. An improvement in our system this year allows our Algebra and pre-Algebra teachers to be in charge of after school time. Watching this everyday has helped us make good decisions about what parts of our program can be improved upon each year.

Maximizing the potential that math computer software offers in the area of extra help is an exciting challenge. Last year we experimented with 10 seventh graders and 10 eighth graders during our lab time. Two days per week they were with a math teacher discussing a difficult concept. The other three days they were taking a complete online seventh grade or eighth grade math course. We used the same math course our students would take in summer school if they had failed math. In reality, these students had two math classes last year, one online and the other with their regular teacher. The results on their achievement tests were encouraging. Six of the twenty students moved from below proficient to *advanced* in math. Thirteen of the twenty students showed gains ranging from 10-86 points. A visiting director of schools told me last week he was putting all of his eighth graders online next year. He bought several portable labs and paid $43 per child for a software program. The teachers would still facilitate, but the software would drive the curriculum. We are experimenting with placing four or five computers in some math classes to see if we can have extra help readily available for students. Our next goal is to find a math software package or online curriculum that correlates with the state standards and has built-in extra help that is easy for teachers and students to use.

Recently, my wife, a high school guidance counselor, was going through records of her seniors at the end of the first semester. She read directly from student transcripts and math clearly was their biggest obstacle. One transcript read "Failed Algebra (40); Repeated Algebra (51)." Can you hear the implied "If you try harder, then you will be able to slam dunk that basketball"? Are we expecting our students to miraculously develop math skills because they are a few months older? In this case, it's not likely anything changed between failing algebra the first time and failing it the second time. At the high school, there were no lifeguards, there was no army of support to help the student *learn*. After all, at the end of the day, isn't that what all educators want for their students?

My wife told me that this student later dropped out—as a senior! We have some good support systems, like credit recovery, for these situations, but they are reactive rather than proactive. If research shows that math is more closely related to innate ability than other subject areas, then why do we not do everything we can to provide as many extra help opportunities as possible? What we used to think was a look of "I don't care" we now realize was a look of "I really can't do it." Every extra help chance that we have created has paid major dividends in student engagement.

Please be aware of one important truth as you process the issue of extra help and extra time. We are not presenting a theory of what *might* happen *if* you try this. We are watching formerly apathetic students respond dramatically. More importantly, these students are responding differently than they did using previous methods to try to improve performance. What we are witnessing now is a paradigm shift in the minds of the students, a shift that, with a little extra help and a little extra time, is engaging students in the learning process. Extra time and extra help are a *must* to making your new system work.

ICU Notes

Re-Do

A second opportunity

I wanted to take a shot and see if the principle behind the ICU system worked. I decided to go to the local grocery store to purchase a loaf of bread. I picked up the cheapest loaf I could find. The bread was priced at $.99. I went to the counter and a high school aged clerk waited on me. I placed the loaf of bread on the counter and laid out $ .53. I took my time and looked up at the clerk, and then he looked at me.

I said "Yes?" in an almost questioning way as he looked at me like he was waiting for something. I said, "That's all I have."

"I'm sorry," he said, "but that's not enough."

"What do you mean? That's all I have," I replied.

I asked him if he would give me the loaf of bread for what I gave him. He then stated again that what I gave him was not enough and I would not be able to receive the loaf of bread.

I then shrugged and asked him "Do you mean to tell me that my $.53 is not good enough to get this bread?"

The clerk looked at me like I was crazy and he could not believe I was staring at him. I finally gave in and let him know what I was up to. "I just wanted to see if you would accept less than what I owed you, because this is what our teachers do with their students everyday."

As teachers, we are the clerks and we let our students have the loaf of bread everyday. We simply comply with what the student wants and take the inadequate amount of money as the student receives the bread. A clerk at a grocery store demands the asking price, yet teachers accept whatever students offer everyday. Stop the Madness! Stop taking fifty-three cents when the asking price is eighty cents, ninety cents, or ninety-nine cents. You will feel liberated when you become a teacher who only accepts quality efforts. Regardless of how you feel about the idea of not giving zeroes for grades, you have to be tired of some of the work you receive. How can you go through your day and keep accepting some of the student work you get? Are you not tired of the worthless efforts by the students? We were tired of it, but now we've set our sights higher. When once we just asked for completion, we've

It *hurts students* to accept **sloppy** or **incomplete work**, so give it back and *release yourself from the pressure of deadlines.*

now raised our expectations to a set standard of quality. We've been able to get to the point where we don't even mention completion anymore. We have much higher expectations of our students now and are able to emphasize quality.

If it is Not Done Well, then it is Not Done at All

Remember: the ICU system of communication will disarm the students and they will do their assignments. What are you going to do with this new change in student habits? Many teachers have gotten in the habit of taking whatever students give them, giving it a grade, and moving on. Giving work back to students to re-do sounds great, but we are fearful of ending up with zilch. Accepting low quality work sends the message that it is okay, even if you give the assignment a low grade. Remember: low grades mean nothing to our high maintenance students. They have gotten in the habit of giving us garbage just to get us off their backs.

"I am sorry, Zach, but you will have to redo this assignment. It is not completed, or is sloppy, and you know I cannot take incomplete or sloppy work." This is a good example of the routine after switching to the ICU system. Imagine giving poor quality work back to students knowing for sure they will return the assignment much improved. The practice of redoing assignments sends a clear message of high expectations to students. Giving work back will make them mad at first; they will beg you to "Please just take this and leave me alone!" Many of our students take the same approach at home and hope their parents will just leave them alone. If they are told to clean their room, they will simply shove all the dirt under their bed for as long as they are allowed to get away with it. All students can learn responsibility, but grading deadlines aggressively is not an effective way. Accepting sloppy or incomplete work hurts students even more than opponents of no zero grading policies say incompletes hurt. It hurts students to accept sloppy or incomplete work, so give it back and release yourself from the pressure of deadlines.

Since the first year of implementing the ICU system is difficult, we suggest you begin the practice of redoing work, but not overdoing it. By the end of the first year, enough work should be given back so that students know the teacher *might* give it back. It is an important practice to start, but it is not important to push this too much during the early transition period. It's going to be hard enough to get in the habit of placing missing assignments on the ICU list, improving the quality of your assignments, developing extra time and extra help opportunities, and changing students' thinking. However, you will be able to increase your expectations by giving back more and more poor quality work each year. The second and third year after transitioning, tweaking, and improving your ICU system will allow you to do things you never thought possible. By year five, the quality of work being turned in is significantly better than in year one. We give back any and all assignments that are not good quality. We allow our teachers to determine what quality level is acceptable in their own classrooms, and we will never develop a "policy" to attempt to define it. The ICU system works best when teachers are encouraged and trusted to make professional decisions each day.

Many students begin high school unprepared for high-level work and then continue to fall behind because they refuse to do their assignments. Students frequently report that they are not required to re-do work to meet standards, which means that, too often, they are allowed to settle for Cs, Ds and Fs. In keeping with comparisons to real life, however, most adults at work would report that they must redo work that does not meet their employer's expectations.

Teacher Talk

"Each high school needs a plan to address the academic deficiencies of incoming ninth-graders. This plan should include a grading system that refuses to let students fail and that insists that they relearn and redo their work until they meet or approach grade-level standards. Each high school must also provide effective extra help to the students who need it most by addressing their deficiencies on a timely basis."

—*Southern Regional Education Board*

ICU Notes

18

Yes, Deadlines ARE Important!

Individual plans for individual needs

One of the biggest mistakes I made in my first few speaking engagements was implying that deadlines did not matter. "My students think they can just turn things in whenever they want," wrote an angry teacher from another school after just three months into the transition. I was a little offended because it seemed to imply that our students did not respect due dates. So how can we take the pressure off deadlines and still teach their importance?

The rule of thumb we use on every decision about the ICU program is "How does it relate to real life?" In the corporate world, when a boss gives a deadline, is it acceptable for several employees to question out loud, "Hey boss, what if I don't get you that report by Friday?" Absolutely not. So why do our students shout this at us daily? The main reason they ask is because most teachers give an answer. Every teacher can and should *respond* to this question instead of *reacting* to it. A reaction would go like "Well, if you don't turn it in until Monday, the best you can make is a B." A response would sound like "Is there a reason you might not be able to have it by Friday?" Reacting to the question, especially by negotiating extra time for reduced points, leaves students in control because they are choosing to simply trade time for points. By responding to the question, the teacher is trying to get at the source of the need for extra time. By asking if there is a reason to move the deadline, the teacher is maintaining control of the due date by using it as an opportunity to learn about the student and what's going on in their life. If there is a legitimate reason for more time (incomprehension of material, other school work, family activity, church, sports, etc.), and if the student is able to come up with a reasonable alternative, like working on the project over the weekend to turn in Monday, then the teacher should be able to individualize the student's due date. Remember, the ultimate goal is for the student to learn the material.

If the student does not have a valid need for an appropriate amount of extra time, then another real life example comes into play. My electric bill this month is $119 if paid by the due date. If it is not paid by the due date, I will owe $125. The electric company adds 5% to your bill if it is not paid by the due date. Although they will eventually cut off your electricity, they never let you off the hook and tell you

"Nevermind, it's too late. We won't take your money now." As a blanket policy, ten points per day is unfair and needs major modification. The ultimate goal for ten points off per day is not related to learning the material, but rather is to meet a deadline. When you take off points so fast, it adds up quickly. It's true that it sends a signal that the student is not in control, but it also sends the signal that the student has NO control and that they are helpless. Once the subtraction of points begins, students quickly decide it's not worth it. "I've already lost thirty points. Just give me a zero."

Having a blanket policy like ten points off per day is in total contrast to treating students individually. Remember the discussion on establishing an IEP for every child? Stop backing yourself into a corner by announcing a due date with an unchangeable consequence set in stone. The most important thing is to strike a balance where the emphasis remains on learning first and deadlines second. Make a professional decision based on the individual child and the individual situation. If students want to compare your plan for them with your plan for another student, simply tell them that you are not allowed to discuss another child's IEP with anyone else.

Most problems with students trying to take advantage of fluid deadlines will occur in the beginning of the program. Recall that a big part of the program calls on teachers and administrators to constantly monitor student assignments. In most cases, students learn that it is easier for them to do an assignment by the deadline than to put it off and have to put up with homeroom teachers, advisory teachers, subject area teachers, principals, coaches, computer lab instructors, and all the rest of the army of support constantly reminding them and checking on them. A desire to be left alone is often all the motivation students—including the most apathetic students—need in order to turn assignments in by the deadline.

If you still think this is a naive way to look at deadlines, consider that we receive over 92% of our projects and assignments on time.

Student paradigm will change, but it doesn't happen overnight.

ICU Notes

19

RESTUDY/RETAKE

Assessing what you've learned

Tests at school should be directly correlated with test taking in real life. Let's begin this section by looking at several tests taken by teenagers and adults outside of school to give us a healthy model to follow.

Drivers license tests, the ACT and SAT, Bar Exam, CPA exam, Real Estate exam, Insurance exam, Sports officiating tests, teacher certification tests, MCAT, GED, GRE: one of the main characteristics these tests have in common is an ability to restudy and retake. What happens if you fail any of these real life tests? Do you restudy the material, retake the test, and then have the scores of the first and second test averaged together for a new, composite average? Of course not, so how did educators dream up this system?

The goal of any test is to assess whether information or skills have been learned. If you fail a test the first time, it's obvious the material hasn't been learned, and accordingly the goal hasn't been met. The real life model for almost any test you can think of is an ability to restudy the material and then retest for the purpose of meeting the goal of having learned something particular. If you take a good look at the list of tests again, you will notice that it is fairly common to fail these tests the first time. Does that mean the doctor who just operated on me may have failed the MCAT, the medical school entrance exam? If you don't pass the first time, you'll be allowed to retake the test and the first grade is thrown in the trash. In fact, you can restudy and retake most real life tests several times.

So why are teachers resistant to this model when it has such a direct correlation to real life? Many of the same teachers who claim the No Zero system will not "prepare them for life" also refuse to allow students to restudy and retake tests. This is another great example of how difficult it is to *see* and *accept* anything outside of our paradigm. Their argument against restudy/retake is "If we allow them to restudy and retake tests, then they will stop studying for the test the first time it is given." Newsflash! Many of your students don't study for their tests already. Making them restudy and retake will bring about the opposite effect, which is, "I might as well study for it the first time!"

Part of our system includes surveying our students to hear their views and

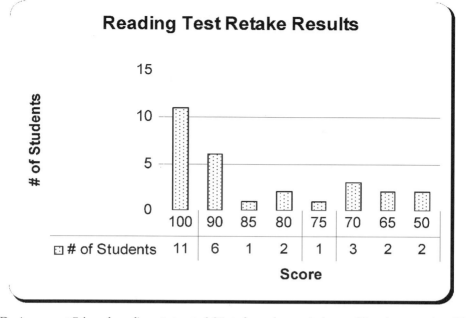

Reading Test Retake Results

Score	100	90	85	80	75	70	65	50
# of Students	11	6	1	2	1	3	2	2

During a recent 7th grade reading retest, out of 27 students who retook the test, 18 students scored an 85 (B) or better. Eleven students made a 100. These same eleven students, on the first test, all scored below a 70. When given the opportunity to restudy and retest, students have a better chance of learning the material than they would if they were given no further support or opportunities.

opinions of the ICU system. Our students tell us that restudying and retaking tests is the best practice we have implemented. The most recent student survey showed that over sixty percent of our students felt they had learned either a little more or a lot more after restudying and retaking a test. More significantly, students tell us they hear the same message they did in kindergarten: school is about learning! And all of this because we use a real life model in testing.

Because we wanted to examine the practice of restudying and retaking tests, we put one of our teachers, Dr. Fred Wheeler, in charge. He coaches a small group of very good students to be our peer tutors. Students who have made below a certain grade set by individual teachers must restudy and retake the test at a designated time during the day. Any student who wants to improve their grade is allowed to participate. This is a work in progress, but it is showing exciting results.

Many schools embracing the practice of restudy/retake simply encourage the teacher to implement this within their class time. This works very well as long as all teachers are on board. By setting this up with Dr. Wheeler in charge, we are able to examine the strengths and weaknesses and continue to perfect this very healthy practice. Last semester, his peer tutors were discouraged after a group of students all failed the retake for a Social Studies test. Dr. Wheeler discussed this with his tutors and found the students were focused more on getting the right answer than on learning the material. The teacher giving the test totally rewrote all of the questions to raise the bar and see if they were truly learning more. If you are going to restudy and retake tests, be sure you maximize this excellent opportunity to raise the expectations of your students and emphasize learning the material.

Be prepared for a small percentage of your top students to complain about this practice; their parents will not like it either. Since we have been preaching the importance of grades for several generations, their children have always competed for the best grades. Their complaint will be totally related to grades and it will be hard to explain the new emphasis on learning. This small group might get vocal at the high school level because of the competition we have created with GPAs. Why should Jenna receive a 98 on her retake when my daughter Kellie made a 98 on the first test? Stick with the emphasis on learning and do not let this small group, although influential, move us away from what research is saying.

As an alternative to resistance to begin with, consider allowing students to re-do/revise/re-take to earn at least a 70 (or the lowest passing grade). This way, they are not leap-frogging over students who did their work or studied to begin with. By year three or four of this grading system, most schools will be able to move to a more pure form of standards-based grading.

Restudying and retaking tests should become a habit of every teacher because it is one of the best tools in teaching students about real life.

ICU Notes

20

WHY DID YOU NOT DO YOUR WORK BEFORE?

Eliminating excuses, one at a time

Now that all of our students are doing every assignment, we have a unique opportunity to get some straight answers and legitimate reasons from former apathetic students. For the past two years, hundreds of principals, directors of schools, and teachers have visited to observe the ICU system. During almost every visit, the educators request an opportunity to question former apathetic students. The first question is always "Why did you not do your work before?" Remember, these students ALWAYS do their assignments now and almost NEVER did their work before. In other words, they have no reason to lie or even twist the truth. They feel really good about themselves and seem to want to help the other schools.

What do you think the unanimous answer is from the former apathetic students? Do you think it is, "I used to not care, but then I woke up one morning and saw 'Just Do It' on a television commercial and it inspired me"? What about, "I used to be lazy, and now suddenly I am a hard worker"? I have now asked hundreds of teachers to guess what the unanimous answer is and nobody has ever guessed what the students say:

"I FORGOT. I am very forgetful, and I used to forget about my assignments."

The next obvious question is "Why do you do your work now?"

To this question, students respond "I can't forget, now. ICU reminds me all the time." Having lots of time to digest "I FORGOT," it has occurred to us that we used to manipulate our students into never using that excuse again. We would preach, "You need to be responsible; that is just not an acceptable excuse." Eventually, students would stop saying it and shifted to blaming the teacher.

Many adults are forgetful. Teachers forget to turn things in to the principal. Principals forget to turn things in to the Director. Supervisors forget to turn reports in to the state. Executives have secretaries to remind them. Some adults have either a paper or electronic planner. Should student success in school be so dependent on their maturity level, personality type, and organization skills? Is it OK to have a built-in system that reminds students frequently?

We now believe that the number one reason the ICU system works so well is because it reminds students daily, and sometimes several times each day, about miss-

One thing is for sure: the students we used to think were just plain lazy or just did not care are now working at a healthy level, making adequate grades, and feeling a lot better about themselves.

ing assignments. One thing is for sure: the students we used to think were just plain lazy or just did not care are now working at a healthy level, making adequate grades, and feeling a lot better about themselves. People worry that the No Zero system enables students. In a way, that's true. The ICU system enables students to remember their assignments, complete quality work, and become responsible students. I whole heartedly support any system that *enables* students to reach such high goals!

ICU Notes

21

HARDWARE STORE

Be prepared

"No Excuses"

I love to run to the local hardware store in town and just gaze at all the items they have. I can go to one of the clerks and they can find exactly what I need to finish any project at home or for the school. This hardware store is a dream. There is a local hardware store in town that has every tool, widget, gadget, and every possible item that a person could need for any project. When it comes to running a school or a classroom, we must create a hardware store that does the same for students—solve all supply and material issues needed. I don't have any paper. I forgot my pencil. I left my books at home last night. All my things are in my locker. We did not have the money to get the project board. I left my folder at my friend's house. Every one of these statements has been used by your students and some are very valid, but many are often a ploy by apathetic students looking for an out. These excuses are still used, but now there is an answer to solve these problems.

When running the ICU you are a problem-solver. You must be able to adapt to any situation thrown at you. Creating a "Hardware Store" is a weapon you build and use in your arsenal to help run the ICU. Though you may think the Hardware Store is a meaningless part of building the ICU, the returns can be invaluable to creating a positive culture, building trust, decreasing excuses, reducing stress, and enabling success. Each classroom and the location of the before-school and after-school ICU programs must be able to eliminate these tired excuses students have used for years. The arguments mentioned above can be one of the most annoying things a teacher deals with daily. Eliminate these worn-out excuses and reduce your stress. Create a hardware store focused on supplying pencils, papers, folders, textbooks, and any other materials to support before, after, or during school help sessions. Make sure there are no excuses in your school. Build your hardware store so that it is easily accessible for students and teachers. You as a teacher or administrator have the talents and abilities to supply a hardware store. Local businesses will not turn you down when you are asking for items for students. Many churches now donate supplies to schools and all you need to do is place them in your hardware store. Pencils, graph paper, project boards, paper, calculators, and other supplies can be

Students should never fail to turn in an assignment or drop out of school because they keep forgetting their pencil.

stored in a storage closet, library office, cabinet in a classroom, or other area in your building. I used to think if we made supplies readily available, then everybody would take advantage and never bring supplies of their own. Actually, students rarely take advantage of the extra supplies, but it feels good to be able to offer. Students should never fail to turn in an assignment or drop out of school because they keep forgetting their pencil. Remember the section on "Speak a Different Language" and specifically asking students "What do you need?" I ask this question frequently, followed by, "Do you need pencil, paper, graph paper, poster board, anything?" Does it surprise you that students almost always say, "No sir, I have everything I need." Please create the Hardware Store, eliminate the excuses, and begin enabling success.

ICU Notes

22

EVERYONE HAS A STORY!

Advisory with a purpose

When I was five years old I had a bike wreck that put me in the hospital in Detroit, Michigan, for two weeks. When I was seven we moved to Nashville, Tennessee, and I entered second grade. During my second grade year, my teacher spanked my hand two or three times each week for either being inattentive or not saying "yes ma'am." In the middle of my fourth grade year they discovered that I was completely deaf in my left ear. Yep, the bike wreck!

The problem with my story was that an important part of it was left behind in Detroit. Had I stayed in the same school that sent me presents when I was in the hospital, I bet someone would have noticed my hearing loss sooner and connected it to the bike wreck. I know I would not have had my hand spanked in front of the class frequently for not saying "yes ma'am," something no one says in the north.

The best part of teaching can be learning our students' stories. Guess what kindergarten teachers know about their students? They know mommies, daddies, grannies, grandpas, who has pets, pet names, which parents are divorced, which parents argued last night, which cuss words were used in the argument, favorite colors, favorite candy, birthdays, who plays sports, and who likes music. The list goes on and on and on.

For the past two years, we have made getting to know our students better a main goal in our middle school, and it has paid dividends. We found out one of our eighth grade boys had just become the youngest certified blacksmith in Tennessee. Two weeks ago, one of our sixth grade boys came to school very upset. Because of our efforts, before the school day had started every teacher, guidance counselor, and administrator knew that D.J. had found his pregnant horse dead in the middle of the night after getting caught in some barbed wire. We already knew he loved his animals, but our communication and improved efforts helped us know what D.J. needed that day.

Getting to know the students reduces apathy more than you'd think possible. It builds into the students a desire to please teachers. Why do kindergarten teachers believe it is important to get to know their students while secondary folks think it is optional?

Advisory that works!

Secondary teachers claim they have too many students to really get to know them; they feel they are just too busy. We have a simple, low stress, no excuse solution. An important part of the ICU plan is to provide a kindergarten-type teacher for every secondary student. This can be done by placing incoming sixth graders with an advisory teacher and leaving them for their three years of middle school. At the high school it even works better, where freshmen stay with their advisory teacher for four years.

One of the biggest problems with the advisory system suggested by SREB is getting teacher buy-in. Although the suggested advisory lessons are good, many teachers end up just reading the paper. Our plan calls for every advisory teacher to do one thing: GET TO KNOW YOUR STUDENTS. We have eliminated all the excuses. You only have 20-25 students to get to know and you have them for three years in the middle school or four years in the high school. We suggest ten to fifteen minutes per day, preferably to start the day. Some high schools do this right after first block. A few suggestions include:

Make a picture of you with your advisory. All of your students will be involved in different activities. Have some type of circle graph around your picture showing who is on the baseball team, choir, band, student council, etc. Even if you don't attend the choir performance, you can easily ask your choir members how the performance went the night before.

Allow your advisory special privileges with your board. Tell them they can write you a note any time on your board if you seem busy and do not have time to listen. We receive notes like, "Got my braces off! — Joslin." The next time you see her, say "Let me see your smile!"

Students love to be measured. This is a hit with the students. Many of our students do not have parents who have marks on the wall to show physical growth. They really do grow over a three to four year period.

Discuss "scars." Everyone, including teachers, has a scar from things ranging from bike wrecks to surgeries to sports mishaps. It is a comfortable and fun thing to discuss while getting to know students.

Celebrate birthdays. Mark everybody's birthday on a calendar. Next to their name write in their favorite candy. On their birthday, call them up, wish them a happy birthday, and give them their favorite candy. It takes less than two minutes, but goes a long way towards having students join your Legion of Support.

These are just a few of the real, basic ideas that we already know the students love. How does this tie into the ICU system? Out of your 20-25 students, you will have only 2-3 students that will struggle with their work. The advisory teacher becomes part of the army of support behind the classroom teacher by checking the ICU list for their kids. The advisory teacher can have their students on a separate contact list so it can be checked in less than a minute.

At the high school level, advisory teachers should serve as a mini-graduation coach and guidance counselor. Every advisory teacher should take pride in having 100% of their advisory students graduate. Guidance counselors and administrators are drowning in trying to keep up with credits, and this responsibility should be shared with the advisory teacher. We need solutions to specific problems when a student starts to slip with their credits, and advisory teachers will become the most important resource in finding out why students are dropping out. We already know math is the biggest problem for students. Advisory teachers seeing this and hearing it from their advisory students could bring about solutions.

How do administrators get everyone on board? Divide your teachers among all the administrators and make every advisory teacher accountable to an administrator. The administrator will stick with this group of teachers just like the students stick with an advisory teacher for their time in school. Hopefully you will be able to have between 20-25 teachers per administrator, including the principal. The administrator must meet individually with each teacher for 15 minutes one time per semester to discuss their advisory. It would be a simple meeting with questions like:

Can you tell me the names of everyone in your advisory? Tell me anything you can about any of your advisory students. Which of your advisory students are on the ICU list frequently? What are some of the things you have done to try to help them? Do your advisory parents feel comfortable contacting you about little things they don't want to bother the principal with? If you have advisory in the high school setting, the most important question is whether all of a teacher's advisory students will graduate, and if not, what can be done to intervene. If a teacher can't name all of the students in their advisory, then this is their starting point—but they had better improve by the next meeting!

Administrators should keep a notebook of these very informal meetings to refer back to. If these brief meetings aren't taken seriously by administrators or teachers, the head principal should keep discussing this with his assistants to be sure they are stressing the importance of getting their teachers on board. The principal will move this forward even more by emphasizing the importance of getting to know your students during at least two faculty meetings each year. Lazy advisory teachers will hurt children's chances for success, and this cannot be allowed. If a teacher is not interested in finding out the story of 20-25 students assigned to them for three to four years, they are not quality teachers and need to find another place to work!

In real life, adults join churches, civic groups, country clubs, and other organizations. The leaders of these groups emphasize getting new members and keeping them once they join. These "real life" organizations place heavy emphasis on getting to know the new members so they will get connected and continue their membership. Another way to look at it is if you join a church or the local country club and nobody seems to be interested in getting to know your story, then you will eventually drop out. Students all have a story. Teachers need to follow the real-life model we see in adulthood by making a sincere effort to get to know each child's story.

It took several years for me to realize the importance of digging a little deeper to get to know our students. About ten years ago, a detective from the sheriff's department came to my office about a half-hour before dismissal. He took me to the gym and pointed outside, explaining that there were patrol cars hidden in five areas around my school. In a few minutes, two of our students would be picked up by their father, who then would be arrested on our campus. The father had been prostituting the fifth grade boy and third grade little girl as he moved one step ahead of the police across three states.

The dad pulled in next to the gym, parked his car, and his two children got in with him just like hundreds of students do everyday. As the numerous sheriff deputies appeared in a flash, I was thankful we could help put this monster behind bars. However, within minutes at least thirty of our staff members stood in tears as we watched the two innocent children get into a lonely squad car. As if she couldn't stand it any longer, our guidance counselor forced her way into the back seat and hugged on them as they drove off.

I learned a lot that day about looking beyond the surface to get to know my students. I wondered, had either of those children ever tried to talk to me—maybe just to say hi—and I was too busy to stop and listen? How many others have come and gone without us learning their story? Is reading the sports page more important to you than getting to know your students' stories? If so, get a nightshift job at a motel and you'll have plenty of time to read!

ICU Notes

23

A WORN OUT '89 BRONCO II
Keeping the kids moving

The fall of 2003 had come and the Bronco was really struggling. We had been together for 15 years and the water, the oil, the smoke, the radio, the muffler, and the air conditioning were all either out of commission or needing constant repair. I loved it! It was my first and I wanted to be with this one for a while longer. I just kept trying to keep it going, but I knew the time was near. I would drive it fifteen minutes and it was time to pour more water in. I had to keep the radiator from leaking so I just kept pouring in the black goo that puts a band-aid on the problem for a few months. Winter was coming though, and without the heater and with a little child on the way I knew it was time. I didn't want to give up, but I finally had to give in. I had put so much time into my Bronco knowing that it required maintenance every six months and I washed it almost weekly. I cared for it and I loved it. The Bronco took me thousands of miles throughout Tennessee, Kentucky, Virginia, and most of the southeast and northeast. This Bronco was family to me and all who knew me knew the Bronco was me.

In your classroom, you have "no maintenance" students, ones who are like brand new cars. There will be another group of students who, like dependable used cars, require "some maintenance." Depending on the overall profile of your school, there will be at least 10 – 15% "high maintenance" students like my '89 Bronco.

My '89 Bronco would break down and I would do whatever was necessary to keep it going. It is very important for teachers to understand this about their "high maintenance" students. Extra help, extra time, and getting to know them will get them going for a while. Maybe a lack of graph paper shut them down for a day, but a packet of graph paper will get them running again for a month.

For years, our teachers would get excited one day because one of these "high maintenance" students was running fine. A week later the same teacher would be defeated and stressed because the same student had shut down again. It will help our stress levels and our effectiveness as teachers to realize that our '89 Broncos are never going to be new vehicles! Expect these students to break down, but trust the ICU system to get them up and running again. The most encouraging part of the ICU system is that it has proven to move the "some maintenance" students into the "no maintenance" group and the "high maintenance" students into the "some maintenance" group. These students need repair almost daily at first because the home situation is terrible. You must pour water in, add oil, use duct tape, add air, and do whatever else you need to just to keep them going. Isn't this what you signed on to do? Did you go into teaching to work only with the new cars? Please do not forget the lesson of the '89 Bronco II. What was once new became dented, bruised, and needed help. You are the mechanic with the skills to fix your '89 Bronco II.

The analogy between vehicles and students is a good one unless it ends the same. Eventually, I had to get rid of my Bronco, but it is not okay to abandon any student for any reason. Are you as tenacious in trying to save your students as you are with your old car?

Two '89 Bronco's

Jason

I cannot believe he comes in with a plan. Jason actually knows what he owes and what he has to do to complete it. He also knows when he is going to complete it. What you don't understand is that Jason is my Bronco II. Jason continually needs the handshake, the compliment, the encouragement, and the time to keep going. If we, the school, place deadlines and use the zero, Jason would hardly every complete anything. He needs the extra time, the extra help, and the extra encouragement. At the end of the first semester, Jason had finished every single assignment and his grades were A's and B's. Better yet, Jason was learning the material and felt like a productive student. Before the ICU system Jason was a student who failed miserably. He did not have a chance following the normal zero-based grading system and deadline process. Now, the way he talks and the way he holds himself has changed dramatically, and it is because of the Power of the ICU.

I first met Jason walking down the hall as a teacher was talking with Jason about not doing his work. She quickly turned to me and asked "What are we going to do? Jason will not do *anything*. He seems as if he does not care at all. What are we going to do with him?"

As I learned more about Jason's situation, he had very little support at home and he had very little support at school. I remember the parent meeting that turned into a cleansing of his locker and everyone agreeing that this poor excuse for organization and effort was going to change. Nothing changed, just the same worn out excuse system prevailed daily, weekly, and monthly. He was the poster child for apathy. Jason had been stabbed so many times by zeroes, teacher frustration, and his own frustration, as well as a lack of organizational skills, that he had given up hope of improving. As the teachers and I talked about Jason's dilemma we came up with the great idea to retain him during the seventh grade year. Nice plan—truly a DEAD END!

The next year started with renewed hope. We tried a change of scenery with different teachers, but skills, attitude, and achievement quickly turned to more of the same apathetic excuses and poor work efforts that we had seen the previous year. The plan of holding him was really working—poorly. We had not changed a thing. We had only changed a few teachers and the year. Then, in November of 2007, we begin toying with taking away the zero and using the beginnings of the ICU system. We had moments of success as we were toying with the ICU system, but we still could not break down all the barriers with Jason and his frustrations. We did not have success with Jason until we had fully adopted the ICU system and committed to every student that we would not quit. Jason is now our poster child for ICU success.

I am so excited to see what is happening for Jason. As stated before, Jason comes in with a plan, a time, and a way to solve his own issues. His self-esteem, his confidence, his success is amazing. Sometimes I just call him to my office or catch him in the hall and praise him for his efforts. He still breaks down from time-to-time, but he quickly solves the problem, reroutes his efforts, and completes his assignments. We are not talking about some of his assignments, but all of his assignments. Jason completes every assignment, many on time, and he has a newly found self-confidence that would make any administrator, teacher, student, or parent proud. The ICU system has turned around Jason's chance at success both academically and as a person. I am honored to be Jason's principal.

Adam

Adam arrived at the beginning of his fourth grade school year with a cold, blank stare. He was not a bully, he wasn't disrespectful, rarely disobeyed his teachers, and was a very good looking young man. His body language confirmed daily a total lack of concern for his schoolwork and grades. Among the apathetic students he was the star! His fourth grade teachers were drained by the end of the year. He arrived in fifth grade the next year due to his age and because it "really wouldn't do any good to hold him back." Fifth grade teachers pulled out every trick they had in their bags of magic to try to get any movement from him. All they got in return was more of the same, or maybe worse, results than the year before: refusing to do many assignments or turning in inadequate work. Adam was again victorious in frustrating and draining the life out of his fifth grade teachers. Once again, he was moved on to the next grade. It is hard to estimate how many times in fourth and fifth grade he was told he would "just have to repeat this grade level if he didn't wake up." All the other students heard the threats, but then they saw him sitting next to them in class the next year as if he had earned his way. Teachers were directed by the principal to move him on because of his age and size. None of the "If you don't do your work, then..." speeches brought any response. He must have been thinking, "I already lost my mom and all my relatives. Why should I care about a zero or if you make me repeat?"

Adam was actually a really neat young man. He had been raised by his mother after the divorce from his dad. He rarely saw his dad who lived in the next county, but he had lots of cousins to play with and aunts, uncles, and grandparents to love on him. At the end of his third grade year, just when his summer break had started, his mom died. How does a child handle something so awful at such a young age? There were even some open-ended questions about the cause of her death to haunt him. At least he had his extended family to hold him, love on him, and give him the security he needed to recover. Who would he live with? Granny and grandpa, an aunt, maybe one of his uncles would take him in. By Adam's own account, "Dad arrived out of nowhere one day and said 'Son, I'd like for you to come stay with me for a couple weeks.' I arrived a few weeks later and was never allowed to even see any of my cousins, grandparents, or relatives who I felt close to."

Now the dead look in his eyes made sense. The droopy shoulders and sad face he brought to school everyday were justified.

Arriving in sixth grade he heard something different, new, and rather confusing: "We will no longer give you a zero. Everyone will complete their assignments and we will give them back if the work is not acceptable." Adam tested the system to the max. As several other students started turning in more work, getting an assignment from him was like wrestling a grizzly bear. By the end of the sixth grade year, he had grudgingly turned in every assignment. He had been pulled during pep rallies, recess, fun days, and occasionally physical education, all of which were his favorite times of the day. He had a teacher right there to encourage him, give him materials, and help him with the tough assignments. He actually started walking a little straighter, talking a little more, and making more friends. Although he visited the principal for discipline a few times every year in the past, he hadn't been sent one time his sixth grade year. Teachers did not hesitate to pass him to seventh grade, this time because he had earned it.

Seventh grade was great, but Adam would still be classified as a "some maintenance" child because he shut down on us a few times. He ended the year with a C+ average and completed every assignment. We raised our expectations during his eighth grade year and he met those expectations. The best moment for me was one morning during the second semester when he popped his head in my office ten minutes before school started. "Mr. Hill—I don't have a printer at home, but I have my social studies report on my flash drive. Could I borrow your printer?" He printed

Teacher Talk

"Speaking from personal experience, it is comforting to know that a system is in place to fill in the cracks, that previously some students fell through. To know the school cares about those students with different learning styles enough to actively seek them out, and offer real, hands-on, help is a blessing to both me and my son. He sees this as a safety net that builds his confidence. This is so important for someone like my son. This program gets my vote."

—Comment from a parent of a student in a school that just implemented ICU this year his report on my secretary's printer and was gone before the bell rang. I walked down the hall thirty minutes later looking for another student and saw Adam sitting in the back of his social studies class looking at me with a "thumbs up." If that doesn't tug at your teacher heart, maybe you need a transplant.

Do you love your '89 Broncos?

ICU Notes

POWER OF
ICU

REAL
STORIES

24

WE WILL NEVER GO BACK

Our priorities are in order

Southside Middle School

Our teachers say, "We will NEVER go back." We began trying to cross over into uncharted waters in the spring semester of 2004. We were tired of student apathy and we desired more from our students.

Sometime during the 2003-2004 school year, a team of teachers and I went to a one day workshop led by Toni Eubanks from the Southern Region Education Board (SREB). She was talking about "Best Practices" to improve your school, and then she made one statement that the team just could not shake. She said, "When you give a student a zero on an assignment or a test, you are letting them off the hook."

"Off the Hook" kept coming up for days and weeks in discussions among the staff. We took a hard look at the thought of not giving any zeroes. We decided to play with the idea for the last nine weeks of the school year by having teachers just tell the students that all work must be turned in or else an incomplete would be given. The students were confused and the staff was encouraged.

During the summer, the entire staff attended a two day SREB conference. Everyone split up into teams and attended numerous workshops related to student apathy, motivating unmotivated students, and discussions with schools already using No Zero grading policies. With lots of fear of the unknown, the staff decided to draw a line in the sand the next school year by saying that every assignment would be completed by every student and that poor quality work would not be accepted.

The next year was unbelievably hard. Students tested the system with stubbornness at first, but habits changed rapidly. After four years of hard work, the students at Southside School do every assignment. Yes, you read that correctly: the students at my school do every assignment. Better yet, most assignments are turned in on time. Teachers have not given a single zero since the fall of 2004 (4 years). By sticking to our guns and never giving in to anyone, a new system evolved.

Southside Middle School has 30% free and reduced lunch children, but more importantly we have an extremely high number of transient students. One of the litmus tests that proves the success of the ICU System is watching new students come in and change. It doesn't take more than a week or two before they get on board. Student discipline problems are so low the in- school suspension teacher now spends 80% of her time as a "Lifeguard" (intervention specialist). Teachers say she is one of the key players in the success of the ICU System.

The bottom line is that the students are doing so much better that it's hard to keep quiet about it. How could we have been so wrong with the zero system? Where did it come from? Who gave teachers permission to send students the message that "you can't learn this now, and it's too late." Southside is a K-8 school and the staff is close-knit. Watching kindergarten students come in excited about learning and then losing the excitement around 4th grade had been a dilemma for years. For years we tried things like better teaching strategies, more individual attention, expensive software programs, motivational assemblies, and lots of parent meetings. Although we had a great reputation in the community, all staff members agreed that student apathy was the number one problem. Now we are 100% sure the problem was that our grading system stunk! The zero system sent a message that said "We don't really care if you learn it." Parents saw the zero as a knife or weapon which led to distrust and arguments. Instead of sticking with the early-grades theme of "What did you learn today?", we shifted the emphasis to "What did you make?" In other words, we, the parents and teachers, unintentionally led students away from the true purpose of coming to school—learning.

We are in shock that the ICU System has changed the student paradigm so dramatically. What is the key to getting there? Why is this being tried in so many schools and failing? This book is being written because Dr. Jayson Nave and Sevierville Middle followed in our footsteps, avoided many of the mistakes we made,

Teacher Talk

"I cannot tell you how proud we are of the school and the teachers. Your teachers, in making this commitment, have really made a difference in students' lives and their understanding of what academic responsibility really is. Keep up the great work!"

—Parent Comment

and sped up the process. In mentoring them, a model of how to recreate success evolved. We feel internally motivated to share this model because it *will* (not *maybe*) positively help all your students.

As this school year started, we were able to raise the standards beyond anything possible in the past. We are playing with several ideas to raise the expectations of our students. For example, if a student is suspended, instead of being excused from assignments, their assignments will be supplemented with extra work.

Think about it—if you are 100% confident you are going to get every assignment from every child, the sky is the limit!

—Principal Danny Hill, Southside Middle School

Sevierville Middle School

I remember bringing a core group of teachers together at the end of my first year at Sevierville Middle. I asked them a very important question. The question was simple, but it was a key point in our development. I asked the teachers, "What is the biggest problem you face in your classroom?"

The answer was "apathy," and they were so tired of students, and some teachers, not caring. The teachers were tired of "slop." The "slop" was draining the energy and professionalism from what they loved—to teach, help, and guide students. The teachers wanted to solve the issue and I wanted to solve this issue for them. We all sat with blank stares on our faces looking at each other as we wondered how to solve this problem.

Then, in the summer of 2007, I was invited to a conference by my supervisor, Dr. Jennifer Younger. This was a time to share with middle level administrators what was going on in our schools and what we could do better. On the last day and the very last session, I decided to go to a segment on the "Power of I." I almost walked out because the room was too crowded, but I turned around and told myself to stay. I stood in the corner of the room, wedged beside a filing cabinet, and I found what I was looking for. Most importantly, I found what our teachers were looking for. I listened to Danny Hill and I heard him talk about his school, his teachers, and his students. I knew right there and then, that this was the kind of principal I wanted to be. You have to understand that I was a new principal without expertise in the profession, without the language of the job, and without experience; however, I loved helping young people. There was an eye opening experience for me during Danny's speech when he said "I love kids." The statement was not abnormal from other educators, but he was openly passionate about his kids in front of all these educators. He got to me that day with his words and his actions and I knew then I no longer wanted to be a part of the stabbing, adversarial process I had been part of for years. I wanted to truly help all students who come into my school and my community. I found what I was looking for, what my teachers were looking for, and it is working today for my administration, my teachers, my students, and my parents.

Was the Power of ICU tough to start? Of course, but through discussion, program ownership, teacher empowerment, and a great deal of communication, the Power of the ICU is moving forward on a daily basis. Administrators, teachers, students, parents, and many around our community know it. The transformation of our school has been dramatic. Through the process of tearing down the old grading system, building communication, providing "extra time" and "extra help," and creating a high standard of quality; our students are succeeding at an alarming rate.

The teachers at Sevierville Middle continually evolve into instructional leaders who now have more time than ever to focus on teaching and learning. We truly feel as if we can develop an individual plan for any student that may enter our building. We look forward to the days ahead and I know we will never go back.

—Principal Jayson Nave, Sevierville Middle School

Both of Us

Both of us are passionate about students, our schools, and our communities. We care about what our students are to become and what they will produce. In tearing down the old, worn-out zero system, we provided our teachers plenty of time and information. In building the new system, teachers were allowed a great deal of input. We now expect a great deal more out of the students and we are seeing great results. The changes we see in student attitudes and motivation are HUGE! The Power of the ICU is real. We love this and WE WILL NEVER GO BACK!

ICU Notes

25

RENEWED HOPE AFTER 31 YEARS

A new reason to teach

Until yesterday, in my 31 years of teaching, I do not recall a single training day that had more than 15 minutes of useful information. However, the training yesterday on the Power of ICU was well-planned and every minute was useful to every staff member at our school, or at least every staff member who is truly interested in really being able to make a difference in kids' lives. This was the first training that I have ever enjoyed. Prior to yesterday, I felt that the idea of getting every student to do every assignment was a great idea, but I did not really know for sure that it was possible. Now I am certain that it is. For 31 years I have been frustrated as I have watched politicians and other non-educators make changes in education that did not work. I have seen these changes come full circle and be repeated. I am on my second circle of seeing education repeat its mistakes by simply changing the name of something that did not work the first time around. Yesterday's session gave me renewed hope that something can be done to fix education. This is so true, how students begin kindergarten encouraged about learning and their parents do as well, only to have this enthusiasm drained by the normal educational process. Requiring the students to complete all assignments as Southside does will clearly get parents and teachers working together. The student is no longer in control. Good parents work together to guide their children through life. They realize that they cannot let their kids play one off of the other. The same must happen between parents and teachers. Parents and teachers will have a whole new relationship with this paradigm. I really believe this is the answer to fixing public education and changing the attitude of parents towards teachers and education. This is something that can really make a difference.

—Computer Technology teacher Steve Book, Sevierville Middle School

ICU Notes

26

IT'S 7:00AM...

Do You Know Where Your Students Are?

I was working in my office doing the daily reminders, getting ready for the day and making sure all information was ready to go for the day when Mr. Cox came in. He came in with a look of amazement, ready to tell a story.

"Can you believe it?" he said. "There are students in the library right now and we didn't even have to go get them. The students came on their own to the library and began working. I had to tell you because I knew you'd like hearing this. I'm amazed!"

I immediately called Danny. It was 6:00am in Lebanon, but I knew he would at least be up and want to hear this.

"Danny—wake up, you ought to be working and at school. We have students in the library and it's only 7:00am. They are working on their assignments and we didn't have to go get them. They came on their own with the PASS program. I had to let you know, for I knew you would want to hear this and I wanted to thank you. There is so much excitement with what is going on. The teachers, the parents, and most importantly the students are with us."

Danny then proceeded to make sure his teachers and supervisors heard my message. "The Power of I" is contagious. This is the excitement that is spreading over the change in attitude and standard.

—Jayson Nave

ICU Notes

27

"I Have Never Only Owed Just One"

Setting goals you never thought were attainable

"Who do you owe? What do you owe?"

"I owe one assignment. I was so close but I don't get to go this time. I will next time."

I spoke with the student in the hall and he was upset that he was so close to getting to go to reward. He was excited that he only owed one assignment, but he wanted to go to reward.

I then asked the young man, "When was the last time you only owed one assignment?"

He then replied: "I have never owed only one. I have never had all my work done. I always owe tons of work."

I placed my hand on his shoulder and said "I am proud of you. Look how close you are. You owe only one assignment—that's great!"

He smiled and knew he was doing well.

In some form, this conversation takes place almost daily at Sevierville Middle School thanks to the Power of "ICU."

The same conversation can take place at your school.

—Jayson Nave

Teacher Talk

"Our first year has been rough! However, we have experienced a dramatic increase in assignments turned in and much improved quality. We are never turning back."
—*Wendell Marlowe, Principal at West Wilson Middle School*

THE NUMBERS

What success looks like

A Need for Numbers

Throughout the "Power of the ICU, " seamless communication, care, extra time, extra help, and a try-try again attitude have been repeated, unfortunately though for so many educators, due to their mindset, they must see numbers in order to quench the thirst for truth. In the next few pages you will see a three-year accumulation of data showing educational growth along with behavioral shifts in the student populations. You may believe that one system cannot create the educational scores or the behavioral decreases you are about to see but, as we have stated so many times, the ICU is a contagious cultural shift and effects everyone in the school. The "ICU Culture" is so very contagious that you will feel a dramatic change in your students. There will be a greater sense of satisfaction and less of a desire to argue or debate over the many issues that you as a principal or teacher are debating now. The change to the "ICU" is a cultural shift that will take over, if you allow it, every part of your school from your teacher, student, and parent relationships, to your behavioral plans, to your entire academic program. Please soak up the next few pages of statistical data looking at math, science, reading, social studies, and disciplinary tactics, and believe that this success can happen at your school. The scores are based off of the Tennessee Comprehensive Assessment Process (TCAP) which is taken annually in the spring of each school year. The disciplinary figures are an accumulation of each schools behavioral totals from the last three years with the understanding that the 2008-2009 school year numbers will be skewed somewhat due to having to tally numbers at the end of March 2009, in order for the completion of the "Power of ICU." For those that "Need Numbers" we believe this will show strong support that the "Power of the ICU" WORKS.

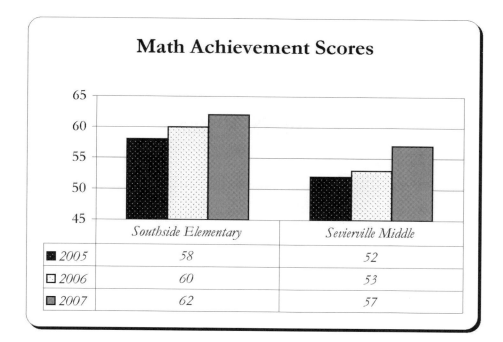

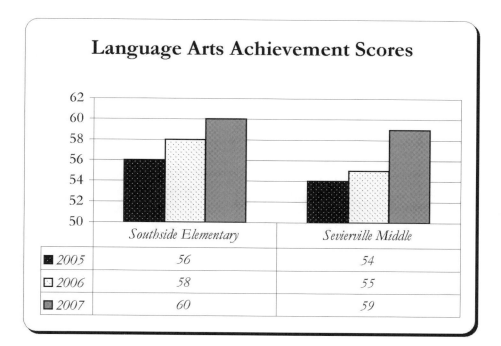

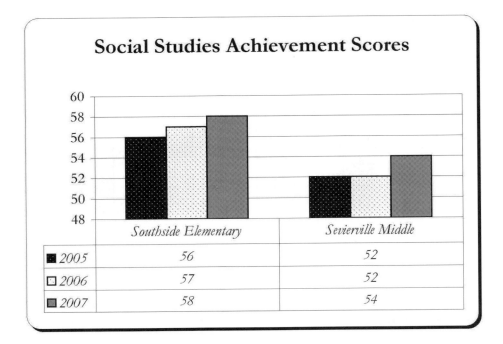

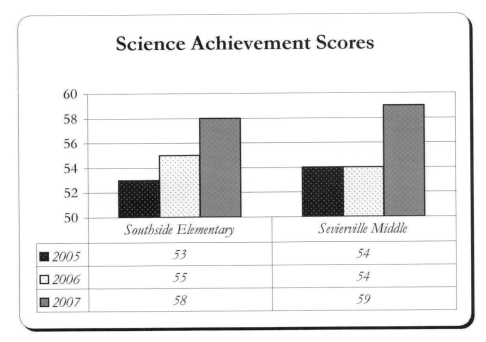

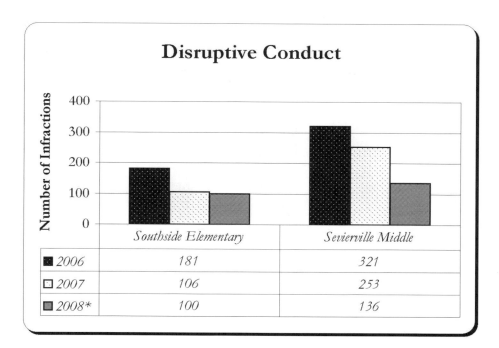

Disruptive Conduct

	Southside Elementary	Sevierville Middle
2006	181	321
2007	106	253
2008*	100	136

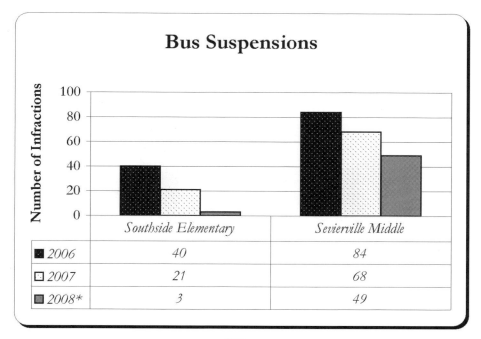

Bus Suspensions

	Southside Elementary	Sevierville Middle
2006	40	84
2007	21	68
2008*	3	49

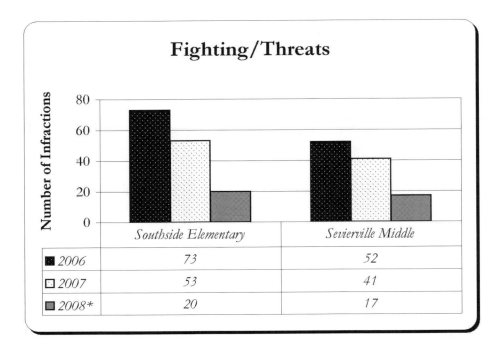

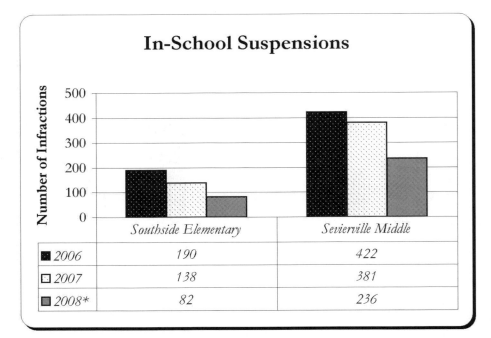

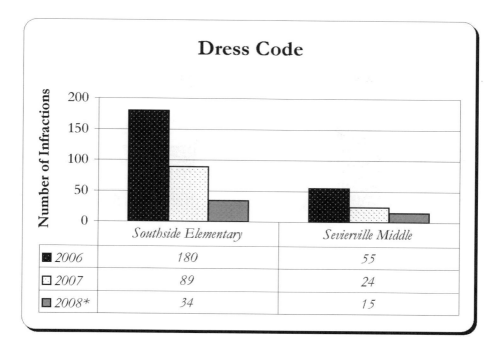

Dress Code

	Southside Elementary	Sevierville Middle
2006	180	55
2007	89	24
2008*	34	15

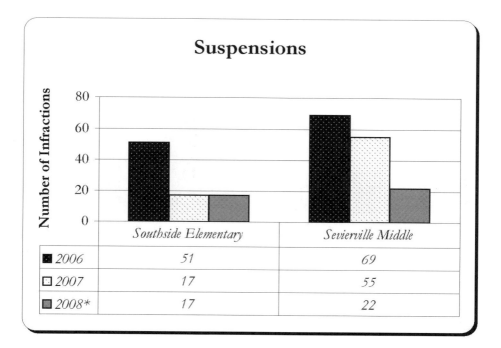

Suspensions

	Southside Elementary	Sevierville Middle
2006	51	69
2007	17	55
2008*	17	22

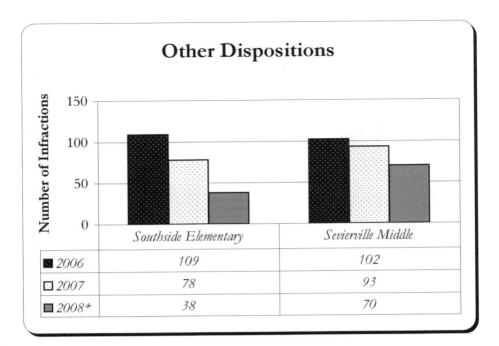

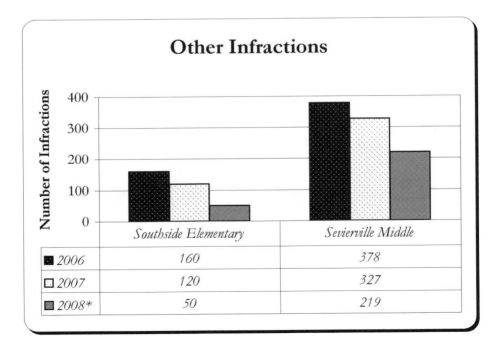

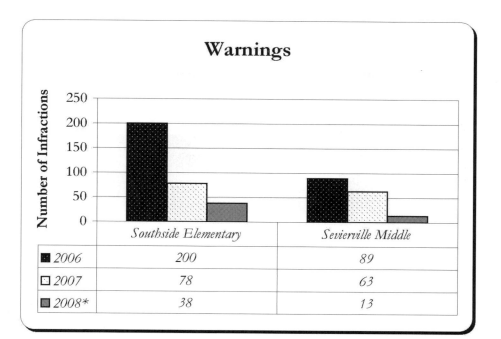

	Southside Elementary	Sevierville Middle
■ 2006	200	89
□ 2007	78	63
■ 2008*	38	13

ICU Notes

POWER OF ICU

WHAT'S NEXT?

29

CLOSING STATEMENTS

This isn't the end

What's Next?

You made it! You have read the book. Your wheels are turning. Where do you go now? The first step is to ask yourself, "How can this apply to my students, my school, my classroom, my teachers?" The "Power of ICU" has to become *your* program, *your* plan, *your* idea. This is not about Danny Hill and Jayson Nave. This is not even about you. This is all about students—so how can these ideas and processes help your students?

Businesses small and big fail throughout America when they try to copy someone else's product without personalizing the message, the product, or the task. There has to be intrinsic desire and empowerment within your staff to make this work. This is the actual beauty of the "ICU" system. The "ICU" is so easy to make your own with proper design, efficiency, and time. Sevierville Middle School runs some processes differently than Southside and Southside runs its system differently than Sevierville due to size, needs, personalities, schedules, experiences, and/or priorities. At the end of the 2008-2009 school year, the following Tennessee schools had initiated the Power of ICU and are reporting positive results already: Crockett County Middle School, West Wilson Middle School, Rutland Elementary School, Watertown High School, Whithorne Middle School, Cox Middle School, Eagleton Middle School, Union Grove Middle School, Clay County Middle School, and Wayne County Middle School. Every school is designing a system that fits their needs.

Though we truly want this to be yours, we do recommend that you begin with two things. The first step is to drop the maddening, knife-stabbing, dead end, suicidal, zero-based grading system and make students earn every point (with time and help on their side). The second integral recommendation is that you must "build an army" behind your teachers and students. The students are in control and we now have a blueprint that works. The shared "ICU" document, when used properly, will empower your teachers. The success you will see in your classroom and your school will be amazing. Also, do not forget to call us or email us when—not if—questions arise.

The "Power of ICU" has to become *your* program, *your* plan, *your* idea.

This journey is not easy, but no great journey or success happens without some strife.

One last word of advice—don't "try" this. If you are just going to "try," then your commitment is too weak to continue building when things get messy. Go for it! Jump off the cliff and never look back. Your students will thank you and your teacher heart will grow healthy again.

ICU Notes

30

Jumpstart Your System

Things you can start today to help change your classroom

The best way to jumpstart your ICU system is to challenge the entire staff to "Speak a Different Language." Type these 7 guidelines on a small card or laminated piece of paper and have everyone tape them to their desks. You will want to begin this immediately and remember that this costs no money and requires no plan; simply begin "Speaking A Different Language."

NEVER...
... use "If/then" threats
... answer "Yes" or "No" when students ask if you're going to take a grade on something. Instead, respond you're concerned with what they're learning and not what's being graded.
... use specific consequences or negative statements when students ask what happens when they don't meet a deadline. Say something like "Is there a reason why you might not have it?" Assume the deadline with your tone and words.

ALWAYS ASK
... What do you owe?
... Who do you owe?
... What do you need?
... How can I help?

The students will hear one voice all day long, every day, and this will have an immediate and dramatic effect on the culture of your school. Can 100% of your staff speak a different language all day, every day? If so, pay close attention to changes in the students and discuss it frequently as a staff to get moving in the right direction together.

ICU Notes

31

THE ONE WITH THE LIGHT

Who will bear the light for your students?

In the early 70's there was a freighter carrying cargo across the Atlantic to ports in Africa. One person on the ship became very ill and the crew worried that his illness was contagious so they sent him down below into a small, dark room, with one bunk, one porthole, and one light. This person was not to come out for anything or speak to anyone.

The freighter came upon a very strong storm that tossed and turned the ship and put the crew and the cargo in danger. The man below could hear the shouts and the yells to secure the rigging but he did not know everything going on. All of a sudden he heard the cry "man overboard." The man below wanted to see but was so ill he could hardly sit up. He kept hearing cries to "throw ropes into the water." The man below got up enough strength to light his lamp and shine it through the porthole. All the man could see was water splashing against the porthole and pitch black nothing. He kept looking and trying to see but the light was no help. Then he heard the sound "we have him." The crew pulled the man back onboard and the first things out of the man's mouth was "where is the one with the light", "where is the one with the light." The crew looked in disbelief as if there was no one here with a light. There was no light due to the storm and the turbulence the crew was dealing with. The fallen man kept insisting "who was the one with the light" and he began searching below until he found the sick person with the light. He came to the sick man and said "thank you" for your light, that tiny light gave me hope. Everything was dark and I was lost but that light gave me vision and hope that the ship was close until I could see the rope.

The moral of the story is that you are the one with the light. You have the ability to provide the light until the student reaches back to grab the rope and swim back.

—from a story shared with the authors by Dr. Bobby Welch

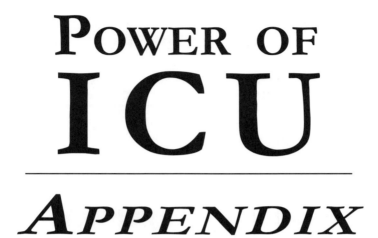

ICU School Culture (from page 35)

What is the School Culture?
in Most K-12 Schools

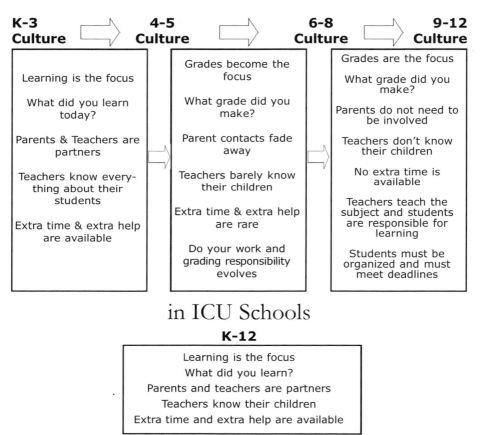

K-3 Culture ⇒ **4-5 Culture** ⇒ **6-8 Culture** ⇒ **9-12 Culture**

K-3 Culture	4-5 Culture	6-8 / 9-12 Culture
Learning is the focus	Grades become the focus	Grades are the focus
What did you learn today?	What grade did you make?	What grade did you make?
Parents & Teachers are partners	Parent contacts fade away	Parents do not need to be involved
Teachers know everything about their students	Teachers barely know their children	Teachers don't know their children
Extra time & extra help are available	Extra time & extra help are rare	No extra time is available
	Do your work and grading responsibility evolves	Teachers teach the subject and students are responsible for learning
		Students must be organized and must meet deadlines

in ICU Schools

K-12

Learning is the focus
What did you learn?
Parents and teachers are partners
Teachers know their children
Extra time and extra help are available

The ICU system creates a culture that is consistent while drastically reducing student apathy. The program seeks to provide students with a consistent culture of learning in schools from kindergarten enrollment to high school graduation. The basic idea is simple: make sure school is about learning from the first day to the last.

ICU Path to Success (from page 53)

ICU Path to Success

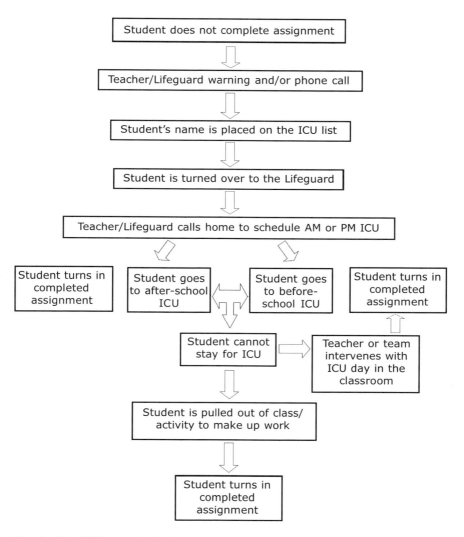

All paths of the ICU system lead to the same end result: every student completing every assignment. The key component of the plan is to provide support at every step of the way, from teachers and lifeguards to before-school and after-school help. After this pathway becomes a part of each student's paradigm, teachers can begin to raise expectations even further.

Three Steps to Creating an Army of Support (*from pages 67-69*)

THE STUDENT ARMY WITHOUT THE ICU

PHASE 1:
In this situation,
the Students
are winning

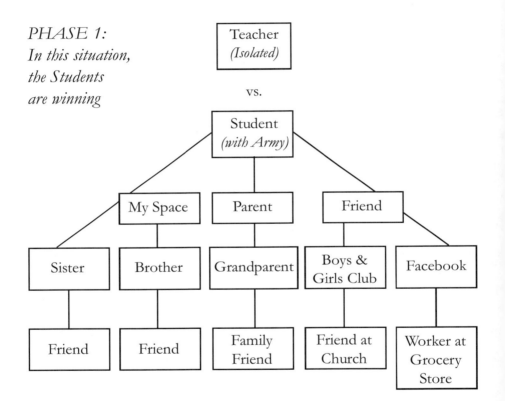

The student builds an Army of Support for their cause that tears away at any credibility the teacher has, making us all question if the teacher is correct.

The ICU will DESTROY the Student Army

THE TEACHER ARMY WITH THE ICU

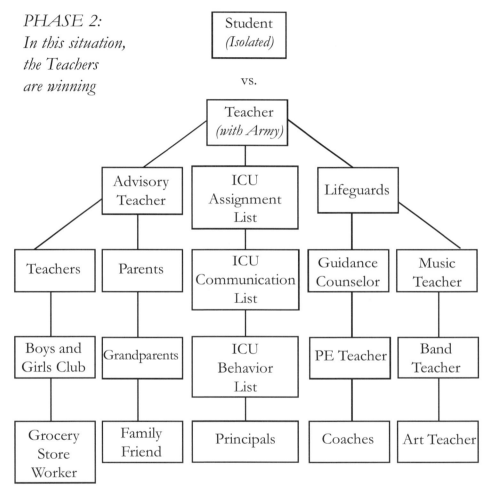

PHASE 2:
*In this situation,
the Teachers
are winning*

Student
(Isolated)

vs.

Teacher
(with Army)

Advisory Teacher

ICU Assignment List

Lifeguards

Teachers | Parents | ICU Communication List | Guidance Counselor | Music Teacher

Boys and Girls Club | Grandparents | ICU Behavior List | PE Teacher | Band Teacher

Grocery Store Worker | Family Friend | Principals | Coaches | Art Teacher

*The Teacher builds an Army of Support that tears away at
any credibility the apathetic student has, and ultimately the
student is left standing alone.*

The ICU will BUILD the Student Army

THE TEACHER & STUDENT ARMY WITH THE ICU

PHASE 3:
No one left
to fight

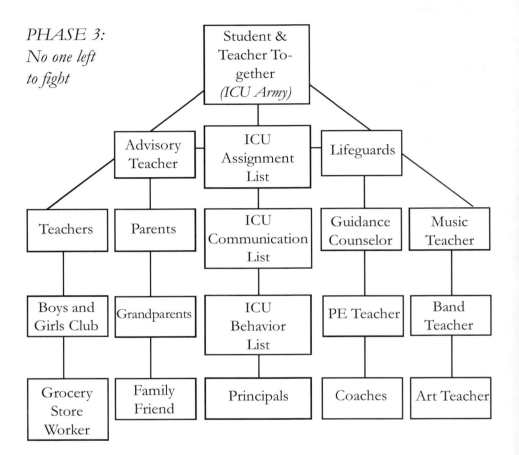

The student is tired of being alone and joins teams with the teacher.
The teacher and student then build an Army of Support together
that creates success and accountability for all involved.

The ICU Army WINS!

Sample ICU Log *(from page 54)*

Student	Homeroom	English	Math	Social Studies	Science
Joslin	Mr. White	Lesson 12, #1-14			
Jenna	Mrs. Jones		p. 124, 1-19 odd		Life cycle diagram
Zach	Mrs. Smith		p. 124, 1019 odd; Ratio flip chart		
Lauren	Mr. White	Descriptive Essay			
Sam	Ms. Martin			Capitals map	

The beauty of the ICU list is that it doesn't require a special subscription or costly computer software. On its most basic level, it's just a spreadsheet. What makes it useful is sharing the spreadsheet over a school Intrashare network or through a free online hosting site like Google Documents. Visit www.poweroficu.com for more details on how to set up your own shared ICU list or to download template of forms seen in this book.

Sample ICU Contact List *(from page 63)*

Student	Contact Method	Date	Time	Name of Contact	Phone #	Notes
Joslin	Phone	2/2/09	9:45 am	Cynthia (mother)	123-4567	Arranged a.m. ICU
Jenna	Email	2/9/09	3:30 pm	Robert (father)	123-4567	Requested conference
Zach	Meeting	1/26/09	11:30 am	George and Jessica (parents)	123-4567	Discussed problems with work completion/death in the family
Lauren	Letter	2/13/09	1 pm	Parents	123-4567	Requested conference/missing assignments
Sam	Meeting	3/16/09	2 pm	Grandmother	123-4567	Arranged p.m. ICU 3/19/09

Although contact logs are nothing new, by creating the contact log as a shared document, one that can be viewed and edited by any teacher in the building, its power as a communication tool is magnified. For more information on setting up a shared contact log—as well as to download a contact log template—visit www.poweroficu.com.

Test Retake Results *(from page 99)*

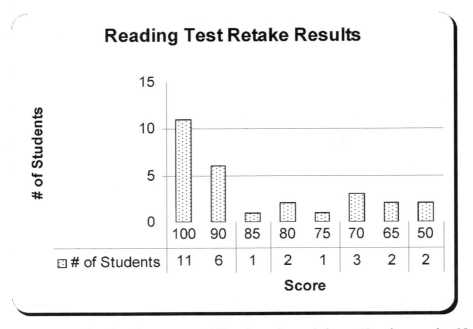

During a recent 7th grade reading retest, out of 27 students who retook the test, 18 students scored an 85 (B) or better. Eleven students made a 100. These same eleven students, on the first test, all scored below a 70. When given the opportunity to restudy and retest, students have a better chance of learning the material than they would if they were given no further support or opportunities.

Achievement Test Scores (from pages 133-134)

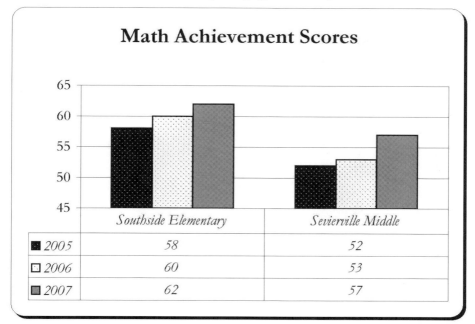

Math Achievement Scores

	Southside Elementary	Sevierville Middle
■ 2005	58	52
☐ 2006	60	53
■ 2007	62	57

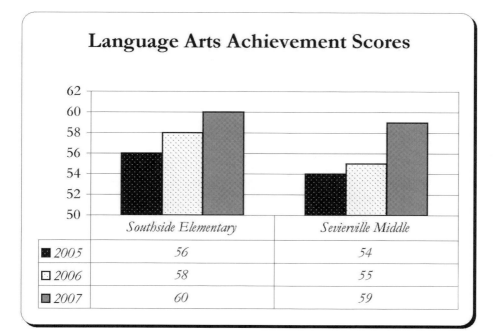

Language Arts Achievement Scores

	Southside Elementary	Sevierville Middle
■ 2005	56	54
☐ 2006	58	55
■ 2007	60	59

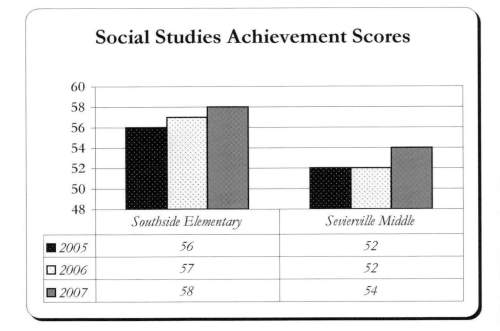

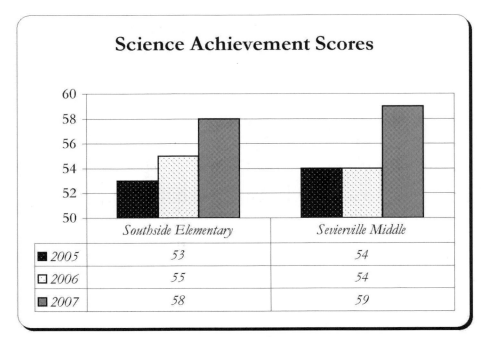

Student Behavior (from pages 135-139)

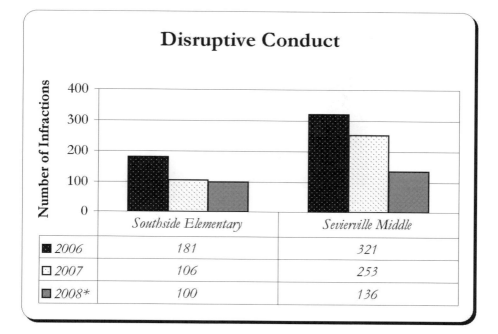

Disruptive Conduct

	Southside Elementary	Sevierville Middle
2006	181	321
2007	106	253
2008*	100	136

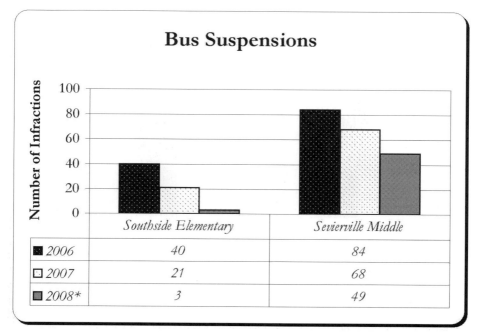

Bus Suspensions

	Southside Elementary	Sevierville Middle
2006	40	84
2007	21	68
2008*	3	49

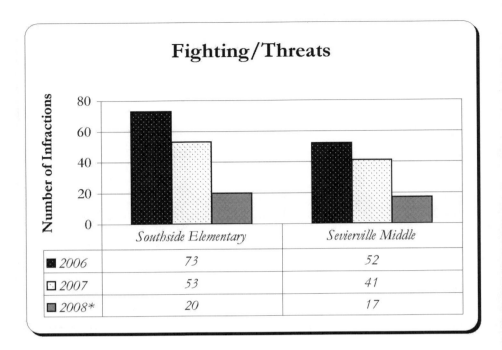

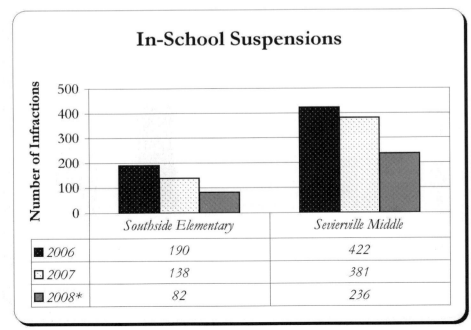

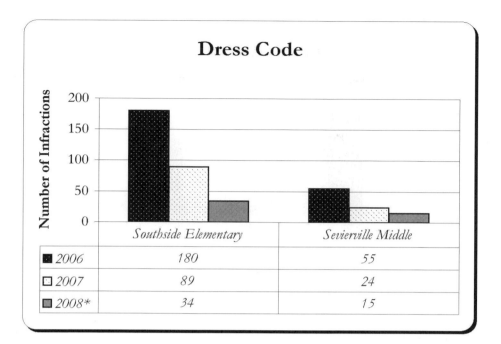

Dress Code

	Southside Elementary	Sevierville Middle
■ 2006	180	55
□ 2007	89	24
■ 2008*	34	15

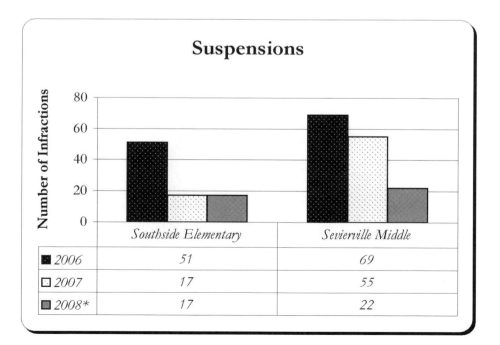

Suspensions

	Southside Elementary	Sevierville Middle
■ 2006	51	69
□ 2007	17	55
■ 2008*	17	22

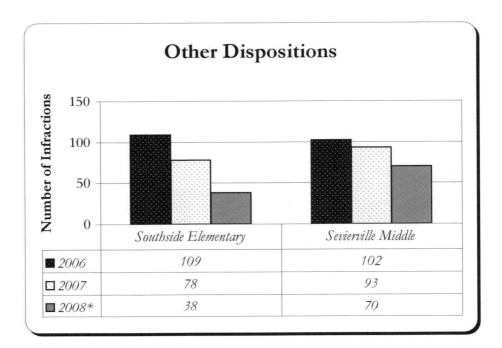

Other Dispositions

	Southside Elementary	Sevierville Middle
2006	109	102
2007	78	93
2008*	38	70

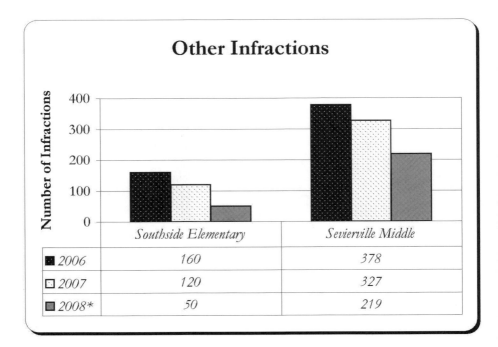

Other Infractions

	Southside Elementary	Sevierville Middle
2006	160	378
2007	120	327
2008*	50	219

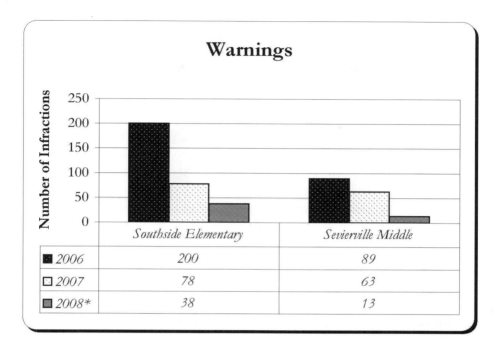

	Southside Elementary	Sevierville Middle
▪ 2006	200	89
☐ 2007	78	63
▪ 2008*	38	13

REFERENCES

References below are cited in order of first appearance in the text.

Lavandera, Ed. "Teachers want to flunk new grading policy ." CNN. 19 Sept. 2008. 15 May 2009 <http://www.cnn.com/2008/LIVING/09/18/dallas.schools/index.html>.

Lucado, Max. *It's Not About Me.* Nashville: Integrity, 2004. Reprinted by permission. All rights reserved.

Southern Regional Education Board. 2009. 15 May 2009 <http://www.sreb.org>.

"Maslow's Hammer," a common unpublished saying attributed to Abraham Maslow

Canady, Robert. "School Policies and Grading Practices that Increase the Odds for Student Success and/or Failure." Principal's Academy. Knoxville. 17 May 2009 <http://www.schoolschedulingassociates.com/canady.html>. All other references to Canady are also from this source.

Raebeck, Barry. "Exploding Myths, Exploring Truths: Humane, Productive Grading and Grouping in the Quality Middle School." Paper presented at the 20th Annual Conference and Exhibit of the National Middle School Association, Nov. 4-7, 1993.

Danielson, Charlotte. *Enhancing Student Achievement: A Framework for School Improvement.* Alexandria: Association for Supervision & Curriculum Development, 2002.

Bernikow, Louise. "Night of Terror Leads to Women's Vote in 1917 ." Women's eNews. 29 Oct. 2004. 15 May 2009 <http://www.womensenews.org/article.cfm/dyn/aid/2048/context/archive>.

Harrison, John C. "Are You Suffering From Paradigm Paralysis?" International Fluency Association. Munich, Germany. Aug. 1994. 15 May 2009 <http://www.mnsu.edu/comdis/kuster/Infostuttering/Paradigmparalysis.html>.

Blankstein, Allan. *Failure is Not an Option: Six Principles that Guide Student Achievement in High Performing Schools.* Thousand Oaks: Corwin Press, 2004.

Ziglar, Zig. "Negative Reactions." Creator's Syndicate. 2009. 17 May 2009 <http://www.creators.com/lifestylefeatures/classic-zig-ziglar/negative-reactions.html>.

Schlechty Center for Leadership in School Reform. 2007. 17 May 2009 <http://www.schlechtycenter.org>.

Ziglar, Zig. *Better Than Good: Creating a Life You Can't Wait to Live.* Nashville: Nelson, 2006.

Whitaker, Todd. *What Great Teachers Do Differently: 14 Things That Matter Most.* Larchmont: Eye on Education, 2006.

Glasser, William. *Every Student Can Succeed.* Mosheim: Black Forest, 2000.

The story of "The One with the Light" cited in Chapter 31 was shared with the authors by Dr. Bobby Welch.

NEED A LIFEGUARD?

Contact Us

In allowing the "Power of the ICU" to take you to a new level of helping, serving, and guiding children there will be times when you need help and guidance. Please feel free to contact us at:

Danny Hill
dannyhill@poweroficu.com

Dr. Jayson Nave
jaysonnave@poweroficu.com

You can also visit us online at www.powerofICU.com for information, ideas, and resources.

ACKNOWLEDGMENTS

Danny Hill

A special thanks to all of the Southside staff I am blessed to work with every day. They make our school a comfortable home and they place student needs above their own. Thank you to Director of Schools Mike Davis and the Wilson County Board of Education for all their support. Felicia Duncan, my elementary supervisor, is brilliant, and she started raising me to be an effective principal nineteen years ago. Dr. Jim Duncan, former Wilson County Director of Schools, introduced me to "Best Practices," the Southern Regional Education Board, and made sure there was money available each year for several teachers to attend their summer conferences. Toni Eubanks, one of the directors of the SREB, is an incredible source of information, as well as a great friend.

A very special thanks to my late father Marv Hill, who was the best man I have ever known, my mom, Darlene, and my two brothers Terry and Dave, who show me "unconditional love" every day. Also, my three children, Kellie, Amy, and Zach, who bring me constant joy. And, finally, Deb—your belief in me drives everything I do!

Jayson Nave

A special thanks to my dad and mom, Charles and Marilyn Nave; my brother Chuck, my friends Doug and Debbie Symonds; Pastors Randy Davis, Jerry Hyder, and Ken Williams who have inspired me through the years. Thank you to coaches Rick Robinson and John Pawlowski for the guidance and support during the days on the baseball diamond, and to Bill Wilhelm for my first opportunity to work with young kids. I also want to thank Professor Terry Tollefson, Director of Schools, Dr. Jack Parton, and the Sevier County Board of Education, and the wonderful staff at Sevierville Middle School, who make the ICU happen every day.

Most of all, a special thanks to my wife Julie and my girls Joslin and Jenna, who encourage me to be the best I can be and bring laughter and love to every day.

Finally, thank you to all the schools that have visited, worked with us, and are now using the "ICU." Keep going, and enjoy helping your children!

ABOUT THE AUTHORS

Danny Hill

Working with children has been Danny's passion since coaching primary-aged children at the local YMCA at age 19. He is a proven educational veteran, having shared his passion for teaching with students in multiple grade levels in Tennessee's Wilson County School System over the past 31 years.

Danny and his wife, Debbie (a high school guidance counselor), have three children: Kellie, Amy, and Zach. At his first presentation on the Power of ICU in 2007, his first session had about 40 attendees. The second session was so packed with teachers, supervisors, and principals that many were standing outside the door listening. A long line of people stayed after the session to ask questions and get his email address. The last person in line was Jayson Nave.

Dr. Jayson Nave

A love for God, a love for family, a love for children, and a love for community fuel Jayson's desire to serve. Dr. Jayson Nave is the principal at Sevierville Middle School in Sevierville, Tennessee, where he is honored to give back to the community in which he grew up.

In his brief educational career, he has been very fortunate to work with ages 7-22, spoken to various leadership groups and schools, and looks forward to serving children, parents, and families for many years to come. Jayson and his wife, Julie, have two young daughters, Joslin and Jenna.

Jayson was in Nashville in 2007 for a Middle Grades Summitt. He was about to leave a session on the Power of ICU because the room was so congested. He decided to stay and saw an educator who felt the same way he felt about students. That person was Danny Hill.